John Newall

Nature's Nobility

Vol. 2

John Newall

Nature's Nobility
Vol. 2

ISBN/EAN: 9783337346423

Printed in Europe, USA, Canada, Australia, Japan

Cover: Foto ©Thomas Meinert / pixelio.de

More available books at **www.hansebooks.com**

NATURE'S NOBILITY.

𝔄 𝔑𝔬𝔳𝔢𝔩

IN THREE VOLUMES.

By JOHN NEWALL.

VOL. II.

LONDON:

CHARING CROSS PUBLISHING COMPANY, LIMITED,

5, FRIAR STREET, BROADWAY, E.C.

MDCCCLXXIX.

CONTENTS OF VOL. II.

NATURE'S NOBILITY.

CHAPTER I.

A HOSPITAL.

THE family at the Close, having settled down after their excitement, Mr. Henry determined to see Tom Moore at the Infirmary, and hand over to him the money and little comforts from his mother of which he was the bearer, and also to leave him a volume of the "Spectator" to amuse him; a work which Mr. Henry swore by, and never went from home for a few days without one of the volumes tied up together with his Bible and Prayer-book.

Accordingly, accompanied by Lawrie, he made his way to the Infirmary. He administered words of comfort to Tom, and particularly exhorted him to serve God and honour the King, and took the opportunity of extolling the virtues of the latter, whom he emphatically declared to be the greatest monarch that ever sat on the British throne, and spoke of his noble presence and gracious bearing when as a mere youth he was crowned King of England, and he saw him on his way to Westminster Abbey on that eventful occasion.

He warned Tom against Radical notions, which, if he did not take care, he might imbibe; for Tom told him how the patients chatted with each other as they lay in bed, and when he added that some of those who had been wounded on the 16th of August were in that very ward, the old gentleman shuddered and hoped that he would not be contaminated by contact with such rebels, and that he should

like him to leave as soon as he possibly
could, and that he would send Joseph
and the carriage with his mother for
him as soon as he was able to be moved
home.

Mr. Henry had never been in a hospital
before, and he was greatly struck with the
order and cleanliness which reigned through-
out.

Tom described how he had been lifted
gently out of the cart, at the bottom of
which he lay stretched on a deep layer of
straw, covered with blankets, his clothes
soaked in blood. How a doctor immediately
attended him, and most carefully examined
the wounds, and extracted the shot,
speaking kindly to him all the while, and
taking care to give him as little pain as
possible—he had been very badly wounded
—and had bound up the lacerated part, and
clean linen being put on him had had
him placed in a nice clean bed (so grateful

to him after the jolting of the cart), and
shaking him by the hand said that he
would see him in two hours, and that,
punctual to the moment, he was at his
bedside ; and how, in the middle of the
night, whilst Tom was in a doze, he thought
he saw some one standing over him, and
waking up, it was the doctor, who placed
his hand on his forehead and felt his
pulse, and, leaving him for a few minutes,
returned with something which Tom said
" fizzed up," and gave it to him, and told
him to try and sleep and he would see
him early in the morning, which he did,
and afterwards saw him twice and sometimes three times a day, and had always
something cheering to say to him.

The old gentleman could not credit all
this, and shook his head in a doubting
way, as if he thought the fever which
had followed the wound had made Tom
imagine all these things. So he asked

Tom if he was quite sure that he was a doctor, and not a parson ; as they always, he said, had a parson at hand in such places (he was thinking of the chaplain of the county gaol), and on Tom saying he was sure he was a doctor, as the nurses all called him "Doctor," he sat ruminating for a minute or two, and then said he should like to see the doctor, as he had never heard of such a one before.

Tom said that it was the doctor's time, and if he would wait a few minutes he would be sure to see him.

And then he spoke of the nurses, and said what good, kind women they were, and how, when he wanted moving in bed, two of them would come, and with the greatest care change his position a little, and if this made him feel faint, as it often did at first, how one of them would run and fetch something to revive him, and how at any hour of the night, if he

wanted something to quench his thirst, he
had only to call "Nurse," and one was by
his bedside immediately, asking him, with
a kind smile, what he wanted, and then,
without losing a moment, she would bring
it to him; and how they treated everyone
in the ward the same.

Tom had just finished his eulogium
when one of the nurses came to his bedside and, curtseying to Mr. Henry, told him
in a kind manner that she was afraid he
was talking too much. She was a middle-
aged person, of an amiable expression of
face, very neat and clean in her dress, with
a little white cap on her head, and a
pair of large scissors in a leather case
hanging by a long black tape to her
side.

Mr. Henry, in addition to his habitual
respectful manner to the sex, felt it his
duty on this occasion to express his appreciation of the nurse's character by a

kind word and a low bow, which was seen by the doctor then entering the room.

Passing to Tom's bed at once, he could not help smiling at the courtly manner of Mr. Henry to the nurse. He addressed him in a friendly but respectful manner, being much struck by his fine gentlemanly bearing, and said,—

" You take an interest, Sir, in my patient."

" Yes, Sir," replied Mr. Henry. " He is my tenant's son, and a fine good lad he is, though I say it before him, and I thank you for your kindness and attention to him. I hope, Sir, you will not take offence if I tell you that I don't like doctors. I never had one about me and, please God, I never will."

The doctor smiled, for he saw Mr. Henry had his arm in a sling, and said,

" I see, sir, that you have injured your

arm, have you done without a doctor for that ? "

Mr. Henry was taken aback, for he had forgotten about his arm.

" Nothing, sir ; a mere scratch, nothing ; only what they call the clavicle broken."

" Only ! " said the doctor seriously.

" I hope that you have had it attended to ; an accident of that kind is not a thing to trifle with."

" Oh yes ; of course not. I mean," said Mr. Henry, somewhat embarrassed, " not by a doctor—but—but—a man who attends to horses and cows—a man in Bloomfield-road."

" Oh," said the doctor, laughing ; " I know whom you mean ; it is the Bloomfield-road doctor. What did he do to you ? "

" Well," said Mr. Henry, " he pulled my arm up and down till the tears ran down my cheeks, and then he strapped it up in this way," shewing the way in

which it was done, "and then he gave
me what he calls 'red-bottle,' which my
servant rubs in morning and night, and it's
getting well fast, and he told me to keep
my fingers here."

"Capital," said the doctor, "that man
is the best bone-setter in the kingdom;
he could teach us regular practitioners a
good deal, if we were not too proud to
learn from him. The way he has treated
you is a lesson for me. I have had many
broken clavicles under my care, and I have
always had a deal of trouble with them;
more than with a common fracture of the
arm."

Then drawing aside Mr. Henry's coat at
the shoulder, and feeling gently the edge
of the broken clavicle, he said,—

"I see that he has lifted the arm well
into the cup, and then, with adhesive
plaster, fastened the two together, so as
to ease the injured ligaments, and he makes

you add to that ease by supporting your left arm on your chest."

Then turning to Tom, and asking him a few questions, he pronounced him much better, and said that if he had not been so far from home he would let him out in two or three days, but he was afraid of the jolting for so long a distance ; whereupon Mr. Henry said that Tom should have his carriage, and that he would write to his mother to come over and she should go with him.

The doctor seemed much struck with the old gentleman's kindness of heart, and when the latter in spite of his prejudice offered the doctor his hand on leaving the bed side, the latter cordially returned the grasp, feeling a kind of veneration for so fine a specimen of a generation fast dying out.

As the doctor passed down the ward to the rest of the patients, he saw a little fellow, handsomely dressed, with long curls, seated by the bedside of a pale boy a little older.

On entering the ward Lawrie was in great fear lest he was going to see a leg cut off, for his nurse had told him, as they passed the Infirmary, that they cut off legs there, and was much comforted when the master, a fine old veteran, who met Mr. Henry in the hall, and accompanied him to Tom's bedside, said that they did not cut off legs there, but were very kind to the patients, and gave them nice things to eat.

After shaking hands with Tom, and listening a while to his conversation with Mr. Henry, Lawrie stole quietly away, and went down the ward, looking right and left, but all the faces frightened him, until he came opposite to the bed where the little patient lay.

The boy smiled at Lawrie, who stopped

to look at him, and, liking the face, he went to the bedside and sat upon the seat by the bed, which formed a box as well in which the patients could put anything, and lock it up.

He was a little factory boy, and had been hired out by his parents to a mill-hand to help him at his loom. About a fortnight before his arm had been caught by the machinery and torn off at the socket, and he narrowly escaped being crushed to death. He was carried to the Infirmary, and for some days his recovery was doubtful, owing to the shock to the nervous system, as well as the severity of the accident.

Lawrie began by asking him why he was lying in bed, and the little fellow answered by turning down the bed-clothes and shewing him that he had lost his arm, which made Lawrie shudder and begin to cry.

The little patient told him not to cry, and that he was getting well and should soon be able to get up.

So Lawrie dried up his tears, and asked the boy if he had a mother; he replied that he had, but that she beat him a good deal, and so did his father.

Lawrie could not understand a mother beating her little boy ; he had never been struck, and he pitied the little fellow, and putting his hand into his pocket brought out the shilling Mrs. Smyley had given him, and saying,—

"There, little boy, is a bright new shilling," placed it in the hand he had still left; and then he told him what a kind mamma he had got, and how she had taught him to read the Bible, and when the little fellow looked as if he had never heard of such a book, Lawrie began to tell him his Bible stories, and was in the midst of Jonah in the whale's belly when the doctor came to the bed, and looking very kindly at Lawrie, which at once won his heart, he asked him who he was, and was not surprised when he said, "Lawrie de Noel, and that's my godpapa," pointing to Mr. Henry, "and he is so kind to me, he bought me such a big rocking-horse, and such a big fiddle."

Then he shook hands with the little factory boy, and said he would bring him some apples soon, and after the doctor had patted his head affectionately, he joined Mr. Henry, who was then about to leave, guided by a nurse.

Mr. Henry shook Tom heartily by the hand, and bade him good-bye.

His kindness so affected the tender-hearted lad, that he burst into tears, and could only return the old gentleman's farewell by gratefully pressing his hands.

As Mr. Henry descended the steps of the Infirmary, a groom, whom he at once recognized as the Earl of Whicham's, and who touched his hat to Mr. Henry, rode up to the door with a hamper strapped to his left arm and resting on the pommel of the saddle. Addressing the master, who, hat in hand, stood at the door, letting out Mr. Henry, he said,—

" The · Earl of Whicham, Tom Moore's master and mine, has sent me with this hamper of fruit for Tom, and wishes particularly to know how he is. "

Mr. Henry said, " God bless the good Earl your master, Williams. Tell him, with my dutiful respects, that I have been sitting an hour with Tom, and that he is nearly well, and that as the doctor says jolting in a cart will do him harm, I am going to send him home in my carriage three days from now, and I was going to write to his mother to ask her to come over and go back with him—as he will want attending to, for he is very weak, and has just been crying—and as you will be at Whicham long before a letter would reach her by post, would you be so kind, Williams, as to see his mother as you pass through the village on your way back, and tell her the third day from now, that will be—and the old gentleman began to arrive at the exact day by counting on his fingers, holding his cane under his arm.

" Wednesday, Sir, " said Williams.

"Thank you, Williams; and she had better come to my cousin's at the Close. She knows the house, and I will drive her to the Infirmary, and see myself that all is nice and comfortable for Tom. Good day, Williams."

The latter promised to deliver both messages, and respectfully touched his hat, which Mr. Henry returned with that careful consideration for the feelings of those below him in rank which distinguished him, and taking

Lawrie by the hand they returned to the Close.

Lawrie had a long story to tell his mamma about the little factory boy, whose mother and father beat him, who had never read the Bible, and had lost his arm, and that he had given him his new shilling.

Mrs. Robert pitied the little boy with all her heart, and Lawrie and his nurse with a basket of apples and pears and cakes went to the Infirmary the next day, and delighted the heart of the maimed child with the present.

CHAPTER II.

A MAN OF MANY CALLINGS.

BASFORD, placing his wife's arm within his own, bade her "pluck up," and at a fast pace hurried from the spot where he had felled the miscreants.

He first, however, pushed the man who lay with his head and part of his body hanging out of the cart, inside of it. It was by no means impossible, he thought, that the two, regaining their senses, and knowing, as she told him they did, that she was going to the "valley," might by the aid of the cart overtake them, and they walked at a quick pace listening for the sound of wheels.

Basford had left Whicham on the morning of the 18th of August, and had covered a long distance by sunset. He kept bearing to the north-east, and must, as he thought, have passed Crosdale, leaving it to the left. He obtained a bed in a hamlet which he reached about half-past seven, and rose the following morning at daylight, resolved to reach St. Peter's in the Rocks before night. He had thrown himself upon a bank in a field by the road side before encountering the steep road leading to the valley, when he heard the sound of wheels, and looking through the fence saw two men and a female in a light cart approaching in the direction of the valley.

The cart stopped opposite the spot where he was lying down, and he saw the man jump off the front seat and lay violent hands on the female, whom he at once recognised as his wife.

To seize a stake which had fallen out of the hedge, and rush to her assistance, was the work of a moment.

Kneeling that night together at their bed-side they thanked God for the deliverance he had vouchsafed them from the hands of the two villains.

After a walk of rather less than an hour they saw the light shining from the cottage windows in the valley, and after first taking some simple refreshment at the only tavern, they entered the opening in the hills where the road leading to St. Peter's commenced, and began the hardest part of the journey.

Basford had taken the bag from his wife and slung it over his back, but every now and then she insisted upon sharing the burden, and carried it for some distance ; but now they found that neither of them could get over the ground if encumbered with the whole weight.

Fortunately Basford had some stout cord in his pocket. Fastening it to the bag he passed it over his own shoulders and hers, and thus bearing the weight between them they did the four miles between the valley and St. Peter's in less than two hours, and stood weary and footsore under Ebenezer's ladders.

To their great surprise there was a light glimmering in Ebenezer's window, and on Basford calling out "Ebenezer Thorneycroft," the latter made his appearance on the table rock, and said,—

"Who art thou that comest at this hour of the night?"

"It's Richard—Richard Basford," said the latter in a low tone, for he did not know who might be within hearing.

"Come up, man," said Ebenezer, and gave his hand to him as he stepped upon the rock, "and thy wife too—I'm right glad to see her. But what makes thee so late? and," looking at him from head to foot, added ; " in such strange guise ; let us hope there is naught the matter."

" Hush!" said Richard, I have much to tell thee; God be praised we are all safe, but we have gone through many tribulations since we last saw thee."

Ebenezer led them into his house, and in a delicate way told Mrs. Basford that as there was none of the woman-kind there except herself, she must instal herself as mistress.

He was a widower—his wife had died about three years before. His two sons, remarkably fine young men, had left their parental home shortly afterwards, and with his full consent, as they were bent on a military life, had enlisted, the elder in the 1st Life Guards and the younger in the 2nd Life Guards, and both had early attained the rank of sergeant, being well conducted young men and good soldiers, and held in high respect in their respective regiments.

On entering the house they found Ephraim Norman there.

Ebenezer was much pleased with the manly bearing of the young man under the severe test of the trial, and had invited him to spend the evening with him, and in his own impressive and yet kind way had talked to him about his course of life—that it could bring no real happiness to his soul, and though he was suffering the great affliction of having no wife to cheer him in his home yet it was his duty to bear up manfully under it, and not give way to a feeling of desperation ; that many before him had to suffer the same hard lot, and yet had borne up their heads before men, and by maintaining their own self-respect had retained that of others.

Norman had shared Ebenezer's frugal sup-

per, and was on the point of departure when
Basford and his wife arrived, and immediately afterwards left, Ebenezer shaking him
heartily by the hand, and saying, "God bless
thee ; bear up, lad."

Mrs. Basford heard Ebenezer's short
account of the young man, and pitied him
from her heart.

She then set to work at Ebenezer's request
to prepare some supper for herself and
husband. The larder, placed in the cool
rock, was not empty, and in a short time
Mrs. Basford had a substantial meal on the
table, to which they both did justice.

Ebenezer then shewed them their room,
and they thankfully sank to rest on the
clean comfortable bed which they occupied
on their former visit.

The next day Ebenezer after breakfast
told them that he had many things to
attend to that day. One of the villagers
was very ill and he had to see him ; the

horse of another had fallen lame and
that he had to see also; the village conduit had shown symptoms of giving way at
one point, and that must be attended to at
once ; it was reported that there was a poacher
about, and it was necessary that some en-
quiry about him should be made ; a young
couple who had been asked in the chapel
three times must be married before twelve
o'clock ; and immediately afterwards he
had to christen an infant; there had been
a matrimonial difference between one of
the villagers and his wife, and he had
been appealed to ; a young culprit had
been found in a neighbour's garden with
his pockets full of stolen apples, and
he had to hold a court over him ; and
finally in the evening he had a prayer
meeting in the chapel.

Ebenezer reached down from a shelf some
medicinal herbs, which he thought the
sick man might want ; a draught for the

horse ; a good stout stick for the poacher ; a hammer and nails for the conduit ; a Bible, with marks at the marriage in Cana of Galilee and the baptism of Saint John; and last, but not least, a birch-rod for the lover of apples ; and stowing away these various articles as best he could, the birch-rod protruding prominently from his coat pocket, Ebenezer set forth upon his multifarious duties, first telling Mrs. Basford that he should be very thankful to her if she would look after his household matters so long as she and her husband stayed, which he hoped would be for some time, as his house was lonely since his wife had died and his sons had left him.

Basford and his wife felt greatly comforted by Ebenezer's cordial reception of them, for they had only had an opportunity of judging of his character during the two days which they had spent at his house on the former occasion, but what they then saw of him impressed them very much in his favour.

To them he seemed to possess those qualifications which, had he been born in a higher sphere of society, would have made him a man of mark. To a noble figure and fine face he added a singular mixture of kindness and amiability with great courage and firmness. His " Yea was yea and his nay was nay."

He carefully examined into any question on which he was asked to give an opinion before he expressed the opinion, but having done so he was unchangeable.

He never made a promise to another without having first satisfied himself that he could perform it without injustice to either, but once having given the promise his word was his bond.

He looked forward, never backward, feeling that the past could not be recalled and that the present and the future could alone be dealt with.

He was too unselfish to have made much money, yet he was not without means. A good part of the village was his property, and he never was known to press a tenant for his rent ; for he felt sure that only want of means and not want of will would prevent any St Peter's man from paying him his due.

The old man as well as the youth, the matron as well as the maiden, confided to him their griefs and their joys. Ebenezer Thorneycroft never was known to be guilty of a breach of confidence.

One thing was predominant in his mind —the honour of his native village. A sovereign could not have been more tenacious of the honour of his kingdom.

The patient whom he had to visit that day was a young man in whom and his wife he took great interest. He was a native of St Peter's in the Rocks and had married a " Valley girl." He was a weakly-looking man, with a hectic flush on his cheek and a dry cough, and always seemed on the point of leaving the world, but hung on by the slightest tenure to life; staying in-doors if the weather was cold or damp, and then, when the sun was shining and a warm southerly wind murmured gently amongst the sunshine, looking as if he had taken a new lease of existence.

He had a natural taste for painting, and his young handsome wife would clamber amongst the rocks, and pluck from the crevices the beautiful wild flowers of the district, and sitting by his side at the little round table which she would bring out for him, and arranging his paint brushes and colours and the small white saucers in which he mixed the latter, would watch with childish admiration his faithful delineations of nature's miniature works.

They had played together as children, and pledged their little hands that they would be man and wife, and when they grew up—she a fine healthy girl, and he a small delicate man, she never wavered in her faith, though her hand was sought by many of the stalwart young fellows of the valley, but took him for better and worse, and laid her little store of wealth, for she had had a handsome legacy left her by a relative, at his feet, and told him to take it all, and watching over him as tenderly as would a mother over her child, she devoted her whole being to him.

Ebenezer Thorneycroft esteemed and admired this girl exceedingly; it was the pure admiration of a father for an affectionate and dutiful daughter.

He entered the cottage and found the

invalid lying upon his nice clean bed,
breathing heavily. He had been engaged,
his wife said, the day before in copying some
lovely wild flowers at his table at the cottage door, when a sudden change of wind
to the northwards had struck him with cold,
and she feared he was very ill.

Ebenezer took the young man's hand,
felt his pulse, and placed his hand on his
forehead, but said not a word.

He took down a Bible from the shelf in
the room, and, opening it, put his fingers on
one of the Psalms of David, where the royal
bard sang of the goodness of the Lord under
his afflictions, and praised him for his mani-
fold kindness and mercies.

"Read that," he said, turning to the wife,
"to thy husband when I am gone."

Then he took from his pocket some of
the herbs which he had brought, and instructed her how to prepare them for the
sufferer.

Giving her a sign to follow him he left
the room, and she soon joined him in the
little parlour.

"Rachel," he said, taking her hand,
"thou wilt lose thy companion."

She looked mournfully into his face and
burst into tears.

Ebenezer did not reach home until he
had looked at the horse and administered
the draught ;   had repaired the conduit ;
had met the poacher, who was accompanied by a villanous-looking cur, and
taken the law into his own hands by
administering a good thrashing, with a
warning that he had better not make
his appearance in those parts again,
and killing the dog ; had made the young
pair happy ; and baptised the child by
the name of Jeremiah ; had endeavoured
(unsuccessfully) to cure the matrimonial
differences; and had abated the proclivities
of the indiscriminate admirer of apples by

ordering him a good birching, which he inflicted with his own hand, and for which no doubt the youngster felt in after life deeply grateful.

CHAPTER III.

THE days of Mr. Henry's visit to the Close flew pleasantly away. His little godson was his constant companion in his morning and afternoon walks.

They sometimes went into the Cathedral for week-day morning service, when Mr. Henry descanted largely upon the monuments of the neighbouring gentry. He was particularly eloquent on the exploits of the great Earls whose chapel, filled with recumbent warriors, stood at one end of the pile. He spoke of their commanding influence in the county, of their vast estates, of their pride of ancestry, which led them to remain in that rank in the

peerage by which they had been histori-
cally known for six hundred years rather
than merge it in the ducal coronet.

Sometimes they strolled into that ancient
monastic building which we have before
described, where the old librarian, after
rallying Mr. Henry on his youthful looks,
would spread out those manuscripts of un-
told value, the handiwork of the monks, the
former inhabitants, brilliant in illuminations,
and looking as fresh as if they had only
just left the cunning hand which had so
marvellously produced them.

On leaving, the old gentleman loved to
stand with his little charge, looking at the
youthful sports of the quaintly-dressed lads,
showering coppers amongst them, and laughing heartily at their scrambles.

Miss Vandaleur's rooms were so near
that Mr. Henry found it very convenient
to "drop in" in the afternoon, and was
always greeted with a hearty welcome.

The many-coloured china tea-cups and saucers, and the antique silver service would then be brought into requisition, and the worthy little lady, with all the vivacity of the Irishwoman and the prettiest brogue imaginable, would talk of Lord Edward Fitzgerald's rising, and how her cousin, a lieutenant of dragoons, had captured him at the hazard of his life, and had been promoted for his bravery, and how her father, who lived in Merrion-square, got on to the top of his house with his blunderbuss to defend the lower part of it.

And then she would tell anecdotes of members of the Irish Parliament, some of whom were her relations; how many duels followed every lively debate, and how a relative of her own in the House, having challenged another member from the same county, it was arranged that the event should come off in the county; and how thousands in carriages, on horseback, and on foot, came

from all parts to see the fight, and how
her relative, having at the first discharge
been wounded in the leg, requested one of
his friends to hold him up for another
shot, which the former agreed to do ; but
a third party, who held an insurance on
his life, unnecessarily interfering, the com-
batant was tied to a tree, and had the
satisfaction of disabling his adversary ; and
how the Chief-Justice had been "out"
with four of the leading counsel of his
court, and all the other judges had gone
through the baptism of fire.

And then she would describe the good-
humoured festivities of the Irish gentlemen ;
how it was considered a grievous insult
to the company if any guest ventured to
take his departure until two-thirds of the
diners were under the table, and how one
night, at a hilarious meeting, consisting
chiefly of members of the Irish Parliament,
one of the company determined to escape,

rushed down a passage leading, as he thought, to the front door, but which unfortunately led to the fish-pond, into which the pursued and the pursuer alike plunged headlong, and were fished out by boat-hooks, and how when they took their seats in the House next day they were greeted with roars of laughter.

Then she would descant upon the wonderful powers of eloquence possessed by her countrymen, to one of whom, the illustrious Grattan, she was nearly related, when Mr. Henry would gallantly suggest that if they only possessed half her persuasive powers their influence must have been great indeed; whereupon Miss Vandaleur, slightly blushing, would give him a tap with her fan on the arm, and say that he was much too complimentary.

At other times Mr. Henry would spend half an hour with his cousin at his place of business, and think what a wonderful head that must be which could turn from one subject to another, each involving thousands, without the slightest hesitation or confusion, and that just half a day at such work would turn his brain.

At Lawrie's earnest request he had invested in the purchase of a couple of fishing rods, and, accompanied by him and Joseph, and seated on a camp stool, essayed the capture of the finny tribe from the banks of the river, where the green sward sloped pleasantly down.

But on one eventful occasion, when Lawrie had hooked a fish, Mr. Henry's excitement became so great that he snatched the fishing rod from Lawrie, and gave it such a jerk that the fish broke away, and the line, flying over Joseph hooked him in the calf, and Mr. Henry, with the exertion, sliding on his camp stool towards the water, would inevitably have fallen in had not Joseph, with admirable presence of mind and despite the pain from the hook, seized him manfully by the collar, and saved him from becoming food for the fishes he was cunningly endeavouring to entrap.

Mrs. Robert, hearing of this, put her gentle prohibition upon any further imitation of the prowess of Izaak Walton.

So in pleasant idleness the fortnight passed by. Joseph had seen to the yellow carriage, which had not only been put right as regarded the damaged iron, but had had put on it a radiant brightness, all the paint having been cleaned and varnished.

Mr. Henry, the day prior to his departure, had instructed Joseph to order post horses, and particularly reminded him of the necessity of engaging a post-boy as coachman for the day who could get into the garments provided for that purpose.

Joseph, who wanted two or three hours' leisure before leaving Lumechester, expatiated at length upon the time which it

would take to select the horses and coachman, and Mr. Henry gave him the afternoon
for the purpose, simply observing that as
he was not limited to an establishment
like the " Spotted Deer " it would scarcely
take all that time.

Joseph betook himself to the " Royal,"
a great posting house in the town, and
it was necessary, in order to arrive at a
proper selection from the many steeds
in the stables, that he and the head ostler
should discuss the question through the
medium of a large tankard of ale, paid
for by Joseph, and as it was necessary to
consult the proposed charioteer in regard
to his height and width, another tankard
was necessary to solve that knotty point.

There was a large number of horses
to choose from, and it required so long a
time to reconcile the conflicting opinions of
Joseph, the ostler, and the post-boy, that
the shades of evening came on before

matters were arranged; and by that time
Joseph's faculties were somewhat confused
by the potency of the ale.

It was suggested to Joseph by the ostler,
who had an eye to business, that having
regard to his master being a " real gentleman," it would be more becoming if he
had four horses and two post-boys, instead
of two horses and an extemporised coachman,
and Joseph, being then in a very yielding
and placable temper, consented. This entitled Joseph to a tankard of ale at the
expense of the house, and of course he
must take time to drink it.

The evening passed on and still no Joseph.

Tombs entered upon his duties, and had
scarcely done so when he discerned a recumbent figure near the Cathedral Gates.
Turning his lantern towards it he exclaimed, " Why I'm blessed if it beant
oseph." Then raising him up, he asked
if he had been to the " Red Dragon," that

being the only tavern that he could imagine would be entered by any person staying on his beat.

" No," said Joseph, " none of your r—r— radical taverns for me. R—r—oyal's the name."

Tombs giving Joseph his arm, took him home, smuggling him in at the garden entrance, and the servants helped him to bed, concealing his state from Mr. Henry, whom it would have shocked very much, as he had confidence, and justly so, in Joseph's habitual sobriety.

Some days before this occurrence Mr. Henry had confided to Joseph his intention of asking Mr. and Mrs. Robert to let him take Lawrie for two or three weeks' stay at Whicham, and they had talked over this important question from every point of view.

The washing and dressing him in the morning and putting him to bed at night

was solved by Joseph suggesting that
Moore's daughter, Mattie, who had just
left a gentleman's service as nurse would
for a trifle attend to him, and that being
settled, all other difficulties vanished as
between himself and Joseph. There would be
no difficulty in looking after him during the
day, and Mrs. Moore being a good cook,
the puddings and tarts in which children
delight would be all he could wish.

When Mr. Henry first mentioned the
matter to Mrs. Robert she laughed heartily
at the idea of her son being under the
charge of two old bachelors without a
female in the house ; but on Mr. Henry
unfolding his plans she seemed to like the
idea amazingly, as it would give Lawrie
fresh air, and shake off the shock to his
nerves which he had not entirely got
over.

After talking the matter over Mr. and
Mrs. Robert consented, and Mr. Henry was

highly delighted at this proof of their confidence.

So the day before Mr. Henry's departure Lawrie's wardrobe was made ready, and his rocking-horse and fiddle packed up for the journey, and Mrs. Robert, with her own hands, made a silk bag for his Bible and Prayer-book, and a little purse in which she put a bright half-crown, and two one shillings, and a sixpence.

Joseph rose the next morning with an aching head and a sheepish look, scarcely able to look anyone in the face, and had no idea of any order having been given by him at the " Royal " except for a pair of horses and a coachman. Much then was his surprise on going to the Cathedral gates at the appointed hour of eleven, to find four horses attached to the yellow coach, and two post-boys, one of them being the man who had assisted in the potations the previous evening.

"Good gracious," said Joseph, "what is the meaning of this?—I ordered two horses and a coachman."

"Did you," said the man drily, "then I'm afeard you altered your mind."

By this time the unusual appearance of four horses and a large handsome carriage had attracted a considerable crowd, who made divers speculations as to whom it was for. At last they concluded it was "for th' Bishop," seeing that it stood close to the Cathedral gates.

Shortly, Joseph and Mr. Robert's servant appeared with the rocking-horse, which they proceeded to fasten on the top of the carriage, and this puzzled the crowd greatly, as they were at a loss to know what a Bishop wanted with a rocking-horse.

"Whoy," said one irreverent looker-on, "he puts his sermons inside and rocks it up and down, and the one on the top he takes out for next Sunday."

But next followed Lawrie's little turn-up bedstead, with its belongings neatly packed, and their wonder increased.

After taking an affectionate farewell of the family at the Close—and it was difficult to say on which side the most feeling was shewn—and lifting his hat and making a low bow to Miss Vandaleur, who stood at her window, Mr. Henry, accompanied by Mr. Robert, walked to the carriage.

His commanding presence and handsome dress at once struck the crowd, and one man called out "Hooray for the Dook of Wellington," which was taken up by the others.

Mr. Henry was astonished at the four horses, but his good breeding prevented his taking any notice of it in public, and he returned the salute of the post-boys with his usual care, and shaking Mr. Robert cordially by the hand, allowed Lawrie to precede him in entering the carriage, and then entered himself, and they drove off amid the cheers of the crowd.

Mr. Henry, mindful of his promise to Mrs. Robert, had told Joseph to go round by Dr. Smyley's house that he might call there.

Much was the astonishment of that worthy lady when the carriage and four drove up to the door.

" Doctor dear, " said Mrs. Smyley, " here is the Bishop, " and hurried into her room to prepare to receive so illustrious a caller.

As she peeped through the window curtains at the handsome carriage, well matched horses, and good livery of the drivers, she felt more and more convinced that it was the Bishop.

" But how odd, " thought she, " to go about with a rocking-horse at the top, and a turn-up bedstead—but these great people can do anything. "

Whilst she was up stairs, the Doctor's

delight at the idea of the Bishop calling
had been dispersed by Joseph's inquiry
at the door if Mrs. Smyley was at
home, handing to the servant Mr. Henry's
card.

The Doctor had heard of the latter's
opinion about him and of his interjections
at the prayer at the house in the Close,
and regarding him as lost to all moral and
religious feeling, told the servant to say
that he was engaged, but that Mrs. Smyley
was at home, thinking that a half measure
would be the best policy.

Mr. Henry was shown into the morning
room, where Dr. Smyley composed his sermons and hymns, and received members
of his congregation and others on Church
business.

The old gentleman occupied the few
minutes during which he was left alone in
casting his eye over the library, which
teemed with controversial works, and

he thought that he preferred a religion without so much contention to one with.

Mrs. Smyley was disabused by her servant as to the rank of her visitor by Mr. Henry's card being placed in her hands.

"Oh, Mr. Henry de Noel, is it?" she said; "does the Doctor know?" "Yes, Mistress," replied the servant, "but the Doctor does not wish to see him."

Mrs. Smyley, thus still more prejudiced by the action of the Doctor against the visitor, entered the room.

"Your servant, my dear Madam," said Mr. Henry, in his usual hearty way, "just going back to Whicham, could'nt leave without saying good-bye."

Mrs. Smyley inclined her head stiffly.

"Yes, my dear Madam," continued Mr. Henry, "I really could not, I know that I had no right to interrupt the prayers, truly sorry for it, but could'nt help it; thought of little Lawrie being hung because his great grandfather stole a sheep, could'nt stand that, you know."

Mrs. Smyley bowed more stiffly than before.

"Sir," said she, " I cannot hear the most solemn matters treated thus lightly."

"I beg ten thousand pardons, my dear Madam," said Mr. Henry, " but I really did'nt mean it, no offence I hope, have been brought up in good old Church principles, none of your confounded Methodist ways."

Mrs. Smyley bowed the stiffest of all bows.

"Not, my dear Madam " he continued, seeing that he had frightfully committed himself, " that I think you and Dr. Smyley are of that low Methodist way of thinking, only——

" Only what, Sir," said Mrs. Smyley sharply.

Mr. Henry was at first taken aback, but

recovering his self-posession he replied, smiling and bowing at the same time,

"Only if I had the advantage of knowing Dr. Smyley's sermons and Dr. Smyley's hymns I might do better."

"Sir," she replied, relenting, "you begin to talk sensibly. I am not without hopes of you yet—those invaluable books may open your eyes, and the eyes of the deluded and abandoned inhabitants of Whicham— I will make up half-a-dozen copies of each, and you can take them in your carriage, and I trust that the seeds they will sow will bear much fruit. Mary," ringing the bell for the servant, "bring a six volume packet of the sermons and another of the hymns, and put them into Mr. de Noel's carriage, and that, sir, is the little account," producing one for £4 10s. receipted, which Mr. Henry at once paid, and making Mrs. Smyley a formal bow, retired. The bow she returned with less stiffness than before, evidently pleased with having done a smart stroke of business.

"Joseph," said Mr. Henry, "never stop at Mrs. Smyley's door again, even if I tell you to do so."

He had sacrificed his feelings for the sake of Mrs. Robert, to whom, in his manly and honest way, he was entirely devoted.

CHAPTER IV.

RICHARD BASFORD and his wife's apprehension that the two ruffians would endeavour to catch them was not without foundation. The two men, on regaining consciousness, became aware of the severe punishment inflicted by Basford's blows, the blood was streaming from their heads and down their clothes, and infuriated at the sight and with drink, they resolved to follow Basford and his wife at the gallop.

Fortunately for the latter the horse had been so overdriven that, lash him as they would, they could not get the speed out of him, and the fugitives had left the tavern in the valley half an hour before they drove up to the door.

They asked in hoarse voices whether Basford and his wife, describing them, were there; being told that they had been there and had left, they demanded to be told which way they had gone. Their bloodstained faces, hands, and clothes, and their drunken howls, frightened the landlord, and he told his son to fetch some neighbours.

The quiet of his house had never before been disturbed by such men; it was frequented by the peaceful law-abiding people of the valley, and drunkenness or bad language was never known within its walls. In a few minutes half a dozen stalwart mountaineers came to the landlord's assistance, and not before he required it, for when he unhesitatingly refused to say which way Basford and his wife had gone, they became abusive, and threatened him with violence, and the more so when he declined to serve them with any drink.

The neighbours then stepped forward,

and one, a very tall, powerful man, demanded
to know who they were, where they came
from, and what they wanted with the man
and his wife whom they enquired after.

One of the men, glaring at the speaker
like a wild animal, said that it was no
business of his, and refused to answer the
question.

Whereupon the villagers held a short consultation, and the former speaker addressed
them thus : " Ye are strange-looking men ;
ye come here with blood on your faces and
hands, and oaths in your mouths, and look
as if ye had been after no good and don't
mean any. Get ye gone. We want no
such people here. Return the way ye came
and at once," and turning the horse and
cart round commanded them to get in.
They muttered curses loud and deep, but
all the villagers joined with the spokesman
in demanding their immediate departure,
and brow-beaten and cowed they drove

slowly off on the road by which they had entered.

So soon as Ebenezer had departed upon the day's duties, Mrs. Basford began to comply with his wish that she would attend to the household affairs. The house had certainly lost much of the well-cared-for look which it wore during the life of its former mistress; for Ebenezer, after the departure of his sons, had been content with the attention bestowed upon it for an hour or two in the morning by an aged female residing in an adjacent cottage, and, as regarded his frugal meals, he cooked them with his own hand.

Mrs. Basford found, therefore, ample scope for her ability as a housewife; she became busily engaged in cleaning up everything; earthenware and china were hunted up out of corners and cupboards, and tins and pewters were polished up and shone resplendent from the walls

grates, fenders, and fire-irons shewed the
effect of a strong hand; hearth-stones and
door steps were whitened; the beds were
looked to and covered with clean linen;
dingy window-blinds were taken down and
replaced by others; cobwebs were swept
from the ceilings and corners; floors were
washed and carpets swept; tables and chairs
were rubbed down; and, by the time Ebenezer
reached home, such a change for the better
had been effected that he expressed his
surprise, and said that the house now looked
like what it used to be.

The day's work had been a sincere pleasure to Mary Basford; she felt a comfort
in having her husband with her through-
out the day, witnessing her labours and
occasionally assisting her to lift heavy
articles. They had not spent a whole day
together in so peaceful a way for many
years.

Basford was greatly fatigued with his

long walk and the excitement he had gone through, and his wife placed Ebenezer's easy chair on the table rock, close to the door, so that she could see her husband as she worked, and there he sat musing on the past, and thankful that a kind providence had brought him in safety through so many dangers.

It was a beautiful autumn day and the sun shone brightly through the chasms in the rocks, lighting up the wild flowers that grew in their crevices, and giving an ever varying light and shade to the rugged sides.

The table rock standing so high got more of the sun than the road below. The rays fell, though with subdued power, upon the front of Ebenezer's house, and so nourished the wild rose, honeysuckle, and creepers that clung to its walls that they nearly covered them. The generous warmth of the sun, the bubbling of the water in the culvert, the quietude, Mary's voice humming some favourite hymn, all tended to soothe Richard Basford, and more than once, his wife, wondering he was so still, left her work, and going to look at him found him in a peaceful slumber. Then, kissing his broad forehead gently, she would return to her work, taking care to make as little noise as possible, and ceasing to hum the hymn.

She thought how happy they might be if Richard would forget politics and leave the smoke and dirt of Drawbridge, and settle down at St. Peter's. He would then be with her all day, and they could have a garden, and beautiful flowers, and keep poultry, and perhaps a cow, which she would milk (for Mary was a farmer's daughter and understood all these things); and was there not that beautiful mountain stream, so pure and so cold, so different to the muddy water they got from the pump at Drawbridge; and were there not the mountains around where they could ramble and talk of the days when, as boy and girl, they strolled hand in hand in the meadows near her father's house.

Richard had not told her of the thoughts which had passed through his own mind when walking from the wooden bridge over the canal to Whicham. Indeed he had not been able to tell Mary in detail all that had taken place from the time he saw her in the attic on the morning of the meeting of the delegates to the time he rescued her from the hands of the ruffians; but he had promised to do so when her work was finished.

When Mary had put the house in order, and attired herself in a neat, clean, cotton dress, she took a chair and sat by her husband's side with her knitting. The sun was setting (the house pointed to the East), and as it sank to the West the rocks opposite were lighted up with marvellous lines, ever changing, ever renewing its wonderful effects.

Of all nature's grand effects, none are so grand as those of the setting sun. Let me take you by the hand, gentle reader, and lead you to some of them.

Come to the Falls of Niagara, that magnificent volume of ninety millions of tons of water per hour. Step with me to the Table Rock on the Canadian side just before sunset; gaze with me on that mighty torrent falling from a perpendicular height of two hundred feet into the abyss below with a force that makes everything around it vibrate; look at the huge cloud of vapour rising from the foot of the fall, where the vexed mass boils and bubbles in struggling billows, reaching high above the ledge of rock from which the mad torrent takes its leap, and you will see the rays of the setting sun lighting up that immense cloud with all the prismatic colours, while birds in gold, blue, and red plumage dart like fireflies to and fro in the mist.

Or, let me take you to the lovely island of Madeira, and ascending to the summit of Rio Grande, 6,250 feet high, look down into that vast cleft, 3,000 feet deep, the Grande Curral, and see how the rays of the setting sun toy and play with its sides before they leave them.

Or, if you are a lover of Gothic architecture, as no doubt you are, stray with me into the Cathedral at Toledo, shortly before the sunset rays leave one of their most beloved abodes. See how the gold and silver, the ivory and ebony and oak, all intermixed by the skilful hands of the most accomplished artists that the world could produce, combine their colours, and ask the setting sun not to take its parting light from them.

Or, if you delight in generous champagne,

we will go to that most comfortable hos-
telry, the " Lion D'Or " at Rheims, and
taking our seat in one of the cozy rooms
looking to the western front of the Cathedral, and ordering a bottle of that delicious wine for which the " caves " of the
hotel are celebrated, we will contemplate
the glorious effect of the sunset rays upon
that most exquisite specimen of elaborate
workmanship, and express our mutual regret at the simultaneous disappearance of
the dancing light of the sun and the bubbles of the champagne.

After all this you will scarcely expect
me to take you to Naples, and shew you
the black mass of Vesuvius transformed
into gold by the gleams of sunset.

Basford and his wife enjoyed the scene,
so different from anything they had wit-
nessed before.

As the sun forsook the gorge, Mary,
whose eyes had been fixed on the beau-

tiful colours on the opposite rocks, took her husband's hand and said, " Richard was not that lovely ; how charming are God's works."

One beautiful afternoon in the early summer, we had been standing on the terrace at Richmond gazing with admiration at the enchanting view, and were about to leave it when, just as we reached the Eastern end, three strolling minstrels turned off the road on to the terrace. Two were young men, the third was a girl with a face much superior to her class, but bearing evident marks of the ´ life she was leading. The men were in advance. As soon as the full view of the landscape burst upon the girl she stood entranced, whilst the tears traced each other down her swarthy cheek.

" This is lovely, aint it?" she exclaimed, with a deep sigh. What could be a greater tribute to the glorious works of God than

that this child of sin should thus acknow-
ledge their beauty?

Basford then told his wife his adventures.
When he spoke of his fearful leap from
the window in Wellgate-court, Mary Basford clung to his arm as if she were holding
him back, and when he told her of the
thoughts that passed through his mind when
he passed through the pleasant country
between the canal and Whicham she took
his hand and said,—

"Oh, Richard, I have been thinking the
same thing. Can't we stay here, or in
Evendale, away from those dreadful fac-
tories, and all the drunkenness and vice of
Drawbridge.

"Think of yourself—think of me—thou
canst not change their nature any more than
thou canst change the leopard's spots. Look
what thou hast gone through for years past,
hunted from place to place, and imprisoned
for what thou callest the rights of man.

"Oh! think, Richard, that there are better and holier things than speaking at meetings and leaving pamphlets at people's houses."

Richard was overcome; he took his wife to his bosom and wept. She did not press him any further, but turned the conversation.

They both felt that evening an inward peace they had long been strangers to. When darkness came on she helped her husband to rise from his chair, for his joints were sore and stiff with the leap and the long walk, and he could with difficulty stand upright.

Ebenezer came home later than usual, and merely stayed whilst Mrs. Basford made him a refreshing cup of tea. He had the prayer meeting yet to attend, and saying that he should be back to supper at eight o'clock went to his duty.

To his surprise and delight Ephraim

Norman was there. There was a goodly attendance at the little chapel, and after a fervent prayer from Ebenezer and the evening hymn the congregation broke up.

The lights shone from Ebenezer's window as he ascended the ladders, and as he opened the door a bright fire and a clean hearth (the mountain air was cold at night) made Ebenezer quite pleased at the comfortable look of the house.

The wooden table was covered with a snow-white cloth, the knives and forks and plates with unknown shine upon them were arranged on the table, and simmering on the hob was a savoury stew ready to be served up.

Mrs. Basford was an adept at cooking, having been brought up by her mother to do something better than read indifferent novels, and strum on a ricketty piano.

The sparkling water from the spring, which Mrs. Basford could never praise sufficiently, was their beverage. After the cloth was removed, Mrs. Basford left the room to clear away the supper things, and make some household arrangements. Ebenezer proposed a pipe, to which Basford was nothing loth, for he regarded it as one of the great comforts of life, and so did Ebenezer himself.

We cannot join in the praises of the so-called fragrant weed.

We once read a story of an eminent man being asked to take a pinch of snuff. "Sir," he replied, "if heaven had intended my nose for a dust-bin he would have turned it upside down." So we may say that if Providence had intended our mouth for a chimney he would have made a vent-hole at the back of our head.

However, we have no right to quarrel with those who hold a different opinion.

Ebenezer and Basford having lighted their pipes, their conversation naturally

turned on the events of the last few days.
The latter told of the oppressed state
of the labouring classes, and the sufferings
which, from want of work and the high price
of provisions, they were then undergoing;
and spoke of the landowners and capitalists,
and the power they wielded over the working
man; but his observations about the landlords were much less bitter than formerly.
Then he explained to Ebenezer the coun-
teracting power of the trades-unions, and
their numbers and influence in the manufacturing districts, and this led to the
monster meeting at Lumechester, and the
part Basford had taken in it, and his
adventures since, but he took care not to
say that a warrant was out against him,
as a knowlege of that by Ebenezer might
criminate the latter for harbouring him.

As Basford proceeded in his narrative,
Ebenezer, always attentive, became more
and more absorbed in the story. When

it was finished Ebenezer slowly drew his pipe from his mouth and said,—

"Richard Basford, I like thee—I always liked thee. Thou art a godfearing, honest man, and as a mother leans to her children so dost thou to thy fellow-creatures. Thou art what the world calls a "patriot" in its best and holiest sense; falsehood finds no shelter in thy heart; oppression thou would'st stamp out; but, Richard, falsehood and oppression are strong—they are rampant in the world—they stand forth dressed in purple and fine linen, and the mighty are their followers. Thou would'st put virtue and honesty and good-will to men on a big pedestal, and tell all people to bow down and worship them. But Richard, even the Bible tells us how man preys on his fellow man. Did not Laban try to over-reach Jacob when Jacob worked as a servant to win Laban's daughter for his wife?"

" I fear me, Richard, that thou hast engaged
in a work above thy powers ; and the very
men who pretend to work with thee drag
thee a step backwards for every step thou
takest forward. All great changes come
from men far above thee and me.

" England would be a papist country
now if bluff King Harry had'nt wanted
to change his wife and the pope wouldn't
hear of it, and America would not have
won independence if George Washington,
gentleman by birth and large landed proprietor, had not gone to the fore. Depend
upon it these landlords and these capitalists are too strong for thee.

"The time will come, and that before long,
when the great ones of the land will join
with the working-man to root out oppression, and then, and not until then, will
their hopes and wishes be fulfilled.

"For the present thou can'st neither keep
the right nor prevent the wrong, but wilt

worry and harass thyself to death in what is now a hopeless cause. "

Then he paused, and continued : "There is one thing, Richard, I would beg of thee ; do not, so long as thou stayest under my roof, and right glad I am to have thee and thy wife here, let out thy views on these matters.

" We don't know, and don't want to know, anything about the rights of man here. George III. may be King of England but I am king here, and we don't want any of your judges, or justices, or constables, or tax-collectors to intermeddle with us.

" I send to somebody at Crosdale what ought to be paid to the King according to my notions, and I hear no more about it, and if any tax-collecting fellow were to come here I'd put him in the gaol and keep him there.

" So long as we keep quiet and manage our own affairs as we now do, and don't intermeddle with others, we shall be all right, but if we get into politics we shall have somebody interfering."

Basford readily gave the promise to abstain from politics; indeed he began himself to feel great relief from the few days of abstention from his absorbing pursuit which he had already enjoyed, and when his wife joined them he laughingly told her of the promise, and Mary thanked Ebenezer for his good advice, and said how happy she should be if she never heard another word about " the rights of man."

CHAPTER V.

The arrival of a carriage and four at Whicham created quite a sensation, and at first it was supposed that it was the Earl himself returning from some weeks' absence.

But seeing the rocking-horse and turn-up bedstead on the top of the carriage, and then recognizing the carriage itself, the villagers were equally pleased to know that it contained Mr. Henry.

As it drove up to Mr. Henry's quarters, Joseph, from the box, condescended to give slight signs of recognition to his friends.

The only person who exhibited any want of enthusiasm was the landlord of the "Spotted Deer," who bit his nails with

vexation at the sight of the four fine
horses and neat liveries, knowing that the
"Spotted Deer" had lost the benefit of 3s.
per mile, besides the fees of the post-boys.

It was, therefore, with some unwillingness
that he allowed the hospitality of his
stables to be accorded to the turnout from
the "Royal," but he dare not refuse, or he
would have drawn down upon himself the
wrath of the Lumechester innkeepers, a
class of men not to be trifled with.

Mr. Henry descended from his carriage
with his usual unassuming and affable
air, and handing out Lawrie, and taking
off his hat, said, " My kind friends, this is
my little godson, Master Lawrie de Noel,
providentially rescued from those infernal
Radicals," and thereupon all the men took
off their hats, and the women curtsied
and looked with admiration at Lawrie's
curls and velvet dress.

Mattie Moore was at the door to receive

her little charge and took a fancy to him at once, and immediately afterwards Moore, just come from his fields and forgetting the tiff, came hat in hand to welcome his landlord, and express his great delight that the Radicals had not killed him.

Moore spoke feelingly, for had Mr. Henry been killed he would have had to make terms with another landlord, not quite so kind and considerate, probably, as Mr. Henry.

It was now Joseph's turn to make a clean breast of it. He knew that he would have to do it sooner or later, for Mr. Henry was not a man to overlook the fact that he had paid for four horses instead of two ; so, before cleaning the carriage, he made his appearance at the dining-room looking very penitential.

" If you please, Sir," he said, " it was not all my fault that there was a mistake about horses, four instead of two. I did

order the two, and was coming home after
taking a drop of ale, but the ostler would
pay for another tankard, and whilst we
were sitting over it, he said that a fine
gentleman like you always took four horses,
and may-be, Sir, when the ale got the best
of me, he got me to order four, and that's
all I know about it, and I'll pay for the
other pair, Sir, out of my little savings."

"No, no, Joseph," said Mr. Henry, much
pleased with his old servant's candour,
"nothing of the kind, we are all miserable
sinners, the Prayer-book tells us so, and
Mrs. Smyley says that I am the most
miserable of all sinners, and I begin
to believe that I am, and we will say no
more about the extra pair. And here
Joseph," opening the two packets of books,
"there's a copy of Dr. Smyley's hymns and
a copy of Dr. Smyley's sermons, and mind
you learn them off by heart, Joseph."

Joseph, highly edified by the sight of the

books, but not knowing exactly what to do with them, being rather inclined to put them in the fire as being somehow connected with his kind master being called "the most miserable of all sinners," left the room, and betook himself to his carriage.

Mrs. Moore had not expected Mr. Henry home until the evening, and, though his rooms were all ready for his reception, she had not provided for his dinner, and on Mr. Henry inquiring what he and Lawrie could have for their dinner she was much embarrassed, and said she was afraid she. could give him nothing but hashed mutton, as if she was quite ashamed of it.

"Why, Madam," said Mr. Henry, "what could you give us better than hashed mutton when made by you."

Here Lawrie interfered, and said he did not like hashed mutton.

Reader, do you like hashed venison? I

think that I hear you reply " Yes." Then
let me tell you that hashed mutton
made _à la_ Moore is better than hashed
venison.

Let your cook cut the meat (if South-
Down the better) into long slices as thin
as a half-crown, make some nice gravy
from glaze, add two glasses of brown
sherry, place the meat daintily on the
dish and surround it with a cordon of
diamond-shaped sippets, serve up with red-
currant jelly, and if you don't pronounce
it very nice, as little Lawrie did, then shut
up this book in a fit of indignation.

After Joseph had disposed of the carriage,
and donned his afternoon suit, he was
summoned to a consultation with Mr. Henry
respecting the sleeping arrangement for
Lawrie. Joseph's bed-room was a large
airy room, as large as his master's, and
very nicely furnished and kept, and Mr.
Henry, thinking that Joseph could bet-

ter attend to Lawrie in the night than he could, determined that the turn-up bedstead should be placed in Joseph's room, and Mattie Moore was called in to do what was necessary.

The little bed, when finished, looked quite pretty in one corner, the rocking-horse was installed in the library, and the fiddle was placed on a shelf in the same room.

Lawrie made himself quite at home. Seated with Mr. Henry in the library after dinner, he scrutinized everything in the room, and then, turning to Mr. Henry, said,

"Godpapa, who is that pretty lady who looks at me wherever I go?"

Mr. Henry averted his eyes from his godson for a moment, whilst the tears came into his eyes.

"Ahem—hem—why, my dear boy," and there his voice choked, and he felt unable to proceed, but, recovering himself, said, "that is my—my dear sister."

Lawrie paused for a moment, and could not imagine how so young and pretty a lady could be his Godpapa's sister.

Mr. Henry saw the child was puzzled, and said,—

"She lived a great many, many, years ago—I used to play with her when I was a little boy like you, and she was a little girl like your little sister that you are so fond of."

Mr. Henry had touched a chord in the boy's heart. Lawrie began to expatiate upon his love for his sister.

"Oh! she is such a dear little sister," he said, "you know, Godpapa, that she is a little older than me—little boys always like little girls older than themselves—and she is so good to me, and takes me down to the river with nurse, and shews me the fish, and plucks the flowers in the fields for me, and buys me such nice sweets whenever mamma gives her some money, and she comes and kisses me when I am in bed, and if nurse is cross she won't let her scold me, but says she will tell Mamma of her. Oh! she is such a dear little sister, and if she dies, Godpapa, I'll have her put in a picture like your sister, and hung up so that I can see her all day."

Then they had tea, and Lawrie was highly delighted with the cakes Mrs. Moore had made, and then, being very sleepy, Mattie was sent for and asked him if he would go to bed, and he said he would if Mattie would let him ride upstairs on her back.

She was just about to lift him up when he remembered that he ought to say his prayers, and he knelt down at Mr. Henry's knees, and said the same prayer that he had said at Mrs. Basford's knees; and then, getting on to the stool on which the old gentleman was resting his feet, he raised his mouth for him to kiss him,

which Mr. Henry did with no small ex-
hibition of affection, and patted him on
his head and said, "God bless you my
dear boy." Then he got on to a chair, and
springing on to Mattie's back, was carried
upstairs, and carefully attended to by her,
and left with a rushlight burning lest
he should awake and get frightened at
being in the dark.

About half-past nine Joseph knocked
at the dining-room door, and being told
by Mr. Henry to come in presented
himself with a countenance full of
anxiety.

"Well Joseph," said Mr. Henry, "what
now?"

"Why, Master," replied Joseph, "we've
not brought a woman's nightcap."

"A woman's nightcap!" said Mr. Henry,
"what on earth do we want with a woman's
nightcap, man? It is the last thing in
the world we want here."

"But we must have it," said Joseph, shaking his head mournfully.

"But why?" said Mr. Henry, "do tell me what you want with a woman's nightcap?"

So Joseph proceeded to explain that the nurse at the Close had told him that Lawrie had said that Mrs. Basford had no night-cap on, and that every night since he had been carried off he had woke in the middle of the night and felt whether his nurse had a nightcap on, and, said Joseph, "I'll be bound, Master, he'll wake up to-night and want to see if I've got a woman's nightcap on."

Mr. Henry was about to prepare for bed when all at once he found himself in this dilemma, and could not see his way out of it. He proposed to make up a pillow-cover from the linen-chest into the similitude of a woman's nightcap, but, having neither needle nor thread was obliged to relinquish the idea.

At last, Joseph suggested that he should knock up Mrs. Moore. The family he knew had gone to bed, but he thought he could get her up without offence, and borrow the required article. So putting on his hat he made his way underneath Mrs. Moore's bedroom window, and, by throwing up some pebbles, managed to wake both Moore and his wife.

The former, in no pleasant mood, asked what the d——l he wanted.

Joseph had felt the difficulty of giving any intelligible explanation, and that difficulty was by no means decreased by Moore's strong language ; but, thinking that nothing but perfect candour would attain his object, he boldly replied,

" I want one of Mrs. Moore's nightcaps."

Moore, amazed enough at being dragged out of his warm bed at that hour, was absolutely thunderstruck at the audacity of the proposal.

"Joseph," he replied, "I think thou wants a blister on thy head instead of my wife's nightcap."

Joseph's heart sank within him; the window was being gradually closed by the indignant husband, when Joseph made another appeal to his feelings.

"It's because Master Lawrie will be frightened to death."

On hearing those words Moore stopped the letting down of the window, and Joseph resumed :—

"If he sees me in bed without a woman's nightcap on."

Mrs. Moore fully appreciated the situation and, laughing heartily, got up, and taking out one of her nightcaps, threw it through the window.

Mr. Henry and he were by no means at one as to how the nightcap was to be worn. The former offered a suggestion, and by way of illustration put on the

cap, but Joseph made divers objections
on the ground that it would not conceal
his whiskers. At last they agreed upon
the mode, and Mr. Henry retired to his
own room, and Joseph, by the aid of the
looking-glass, adjusted the cap to his
satisfaction, and got into bed.

In the middle of the night, Lawrie,
half-awake, finding himself alone in bed
in a strange room, rose up and began
peering about in the dull glimmer of the
rushlight.

Joseph, not very comfortable in his new
head-dress, was awake.

Lawrie, seeing a head on the pillow opposite, got out of bed, and, creeping slowly
across the room, stood at Joseph's bed-side.
It was a critical moment, but Joseph was
equal to the occasion. As Lawrie, standing
on his toes, stretched forward his little head
to get a nearer look, Joseph worked himself gradually round in the other direction,

until he lay on his stomach with his face completely buried in his pillow, turning a deaf ear to Lawrie's calls to nurse to speak to him.

At last, convinced by the nightcap that it was his nurse, he got into bed again and fell asleep.

CHAPTER VI.

A DETECTIVE DONE.

GREEN was a very sleuth-hound in following up his victim. He was not satisfied with securing the eleven delegates and the soldier, but he must capture Richard Basford, for whose apprehension a reward of £100 had been offered by the authorities, and this reward he determined to gain. On the very evening of the day on which he had captured the soldier he made his appearance at the Close, and requesting that he might be permitted to have a few words with Mr. Robert, he was shewn into the dining-room. Addressing Mr. Robert respectfully, but in an open, manly way, characteristic of the man, he said that he came to see what information he could gather about Mrs. Basford. Had she said anything about her husband on being released which would give any clue to where he could be found?

Mr. Robert called in the two clerks who had released her, but they could give no information, as they had unbound her and then instantly left her.

He went to Wellgate-court, but the answer to his enquiries was that Mary Basford had left the same evening, without saying where she was going to, and to questions whether Basford himself had been to the place he received the answer that he had not been seen there since the capture of the delegates.

He was thus left to surmise in which direction Basford had gone after his leap from the window. He concluded that if he dare plunge into the river, deep as it was, he could swim, and, as the current was strong, that he would probably go with it for some distance at least before he attempted to land, and that, when he did land it would be on the opposite bank to Wellgate-court, because, on the Wellgate-court side the buildings ran con- tinuously without opening, and the bank was high. The bank on the other side was lower ; but still, until the point was reached where Basford actually landed, there was no desirable spot for that purpose, as no street ran down to the river, and he must have passed through private property, where his appearance without coat and dripping with water would have excited suspicion, even if he could have got through without being stopped.

Green's exprienced eye at once selected the wharf where the "Nancy" lay as the point of landing, and the next day he commenced enquiring whether any barge had been moored there, and was not long in ascertaining that the "Nancy" had been, and had left early the morning before.

He could not learn that any one but the master, his wife, and the lad, had been seen on board ; but, nevertheless, he thought it very likely that Basford had been hidden away on board, for the bargees, as a body, being lawless man, were only too willing to assist others in evading justice.

The destination of the barge favoured the supposition of Basford being on board her, as from the port to which she was making her way emigrant ships to America and Australia frequently sailed ; and what more likely than Basford should try to get on board one of them ?

He thought it very probable that he might catch up the barge at a considerable town about half way on the voyage, which he could reach by coach.

He took no time in sending for Jem, who, he thought, might be very useful, and the two getting on the top of the coach in the afternoon, apparently quite unknown to each other, reached Brassington late in the evening.

Green at once made his way to the canal dock there, and, to his great delight, found the "Nancy" moored to the wharf.

The master was seated on the top of one of the mooring-posts contentedly smoking his pipe, for he had the inward satisfaction of knowing that the lurcher had been so successful on the previous evening that he had ample supplies of game and poultry to last him until his return to the same land of Goschen.

Green was not a stonemason this time, but a happy-go-lucky Jack tar, with his hat stuck at the back of his head, his blue shirt open at the neck, his trousers being wide at the bottom, and at the waist so drawn in that he looked like a wasp.

"Hilloo! mate," said Green, hitching up his trousers, "what port?"

The bargee took his pipe from his mouth and had a look at Green before he said anything.

In the first place he disliked all approaches to the neighbourhood of his larder as inconvenient—he did'nt mind a brother bargee; and, in the second place, he had an especial dislike to all sea-going sailors, as they were anything but obliging when their sailing craft met his as he was trying to work up with the tide to the dock where he berthed on arriving in port, and his feelings were greatly hurt when he was told to get his "old tub" out of the way.

"Well mate," he replied, "what's *your* Port?"—

"Just ashore," said Green "and want a

berth down the river to the second lock—
want to see mother; she lives nigh there."

Now the bargee, though he had been
on the canal all his life, was as crafty as
a fox. From his infancy he had been
accustomed to scent a constable or a gamekeeper from afar. He was well known to
be an inveterate poacher, and every kind
of dodge had been put into requisition by
the squires along the canal bank to obtain
sufficient evidence to convict him. Whatever
disguise was assumed by a constable or a
gamekeeper, he seemed to find him out
by intuition, and would laugh in his sleeve
whilst the other thought he was drawing
him out nicely.

As to his dog, he was as cunning as
himself, and knew the difference between
what was a bait and what was not as well
as if he had been told.

The bargee replied that he had no berths
on board for anybody but himself and his

wife and lad, and that he had better walk there.

Green saw at once that the man was suspicious, so throwing off the jolly tar he put his hand on his shoulder and said,

" Come, my man, let us understand each other. I'm a constable."

" I thowt so," said the bargee coolly.

"I want to go on board," continued Green, and stepping into the aft of the barge was seized by the lurcher by the leg.

"Confound the brute," said he, kicking him to the other side of the cabin, " lie there," and the dog instinctively felt he. had met with his master.

"Fine hare," said Green, opening the larder door, " nice brace of partridges, ditto pheasants, couple of plump fowls, all reared on board the Nancy, of course."

" In course," said the bargee, as coolly as before.

" Well, my friend," said Green. " I

don't want to interfere with your game so long as you don't spoil mine. Is one Richard Basford on board?"

"Dont know him," said bargee.

"Well, well, try to refresh your memory," said Green. "A man got out of the water into your boat the night before you left; he had had a good swim, and was without his coat, dark man, and tall, nearly my height, bit of the Methodist cut about him, you know him now, don't you?"

"In course I do," said bargee "he came wi' us here, and he bowt my old corduroy suit, and left two hours ago by the coach for the port; he's going to Americky from what he said."

The man's manner was so frank, and the little incident about the clothes seemed so corroborative of his story, that Green believed it, and bit his lips with disappointment. The bargee didn't appear to notice it but he did, and, chuckling within himself, asked Green if he would stay and take some roast fowl and baked potatoes which would be ready in about half-an-hour, but Green declined and hastened to join Jem, and the two found places on the last coach for Wilderspool (the name of the port), and got there tired and disappointed about eleven at night.

They went to an inn near the docks much frequented by sailors, and Green soon learnt that an emigrant ship, the " Western Star," was about to sail at noon the following day for New York, and would clear out of dock about ten o'clock.

He saw the agent and came to an understanding with him, and as the ship lay at anchor in the river just before sailing, Green, as a "jolly tar," came on board and looked like one of the crew.

The scene on board was such as may be seen any week in one of our large emigration ports—English and Scotch and Germans, themselves and their luggage all huddled and intermixed together; an old man, seated on his iron-bound box containing all he had in the world, determined not to leave it until he landed on the other side; the stout farmer with his young family bound for the far west and full of hope; the newly married couple, who had left the old people at home to begin life in a new world; the broken-down tradesman with his anxious-looking wife and pale neglected children; and the nervous-looking downcast clerk who had robbed his employer and sought shelter from his crime.

Green was not long in ascertaining that Basford was not on board, and the truth flashed upon him that he had been done by the bargee, so, starting off by the first coach to Lumechester, he left Jem to make further enquiries as best he could about Basford.

Jem, the very picture of a half-starved factory boy out of work, who had walked all the way from Lumechester to get a job, got to know where the dock was which the canal barges came into, and the next day the "Nancy" made her appearance, when Jem appealed piteously for a turn at the unloading and was engaged. He had not been at work more than an hour when the lad and he became great friends, and the former let out that a man whom he described, who Jem had no doubt was Basford, had left the barge about four hours after it started from Lumechester, and had gone in the direction of Whicham.

Jem left off work, being even so forgetful of his own interest as not to ask for any wages, and immediately started by coach for Lumechester.

On arriving in Lumechester Green went to the office to see the Chief.

"Well, Green, any news of Basford," said the former.

"None, Sir; I thought I had a clue to him, but for once in my life I got done, and that by a stupid-looking bargee, cunning as any fox, who put me on the wrong scent, and sent me off to Wilderspool, where I have left Jem to get information."

"What do you think of doing now?"

"Well, Sir, I intend to be off to Drawbridge; most likely the wife has been there by this time, and has heard from him, and is going to join him, or maybe has gone already, and probably I shall find out the direction, if not the place itself. But I think I'll wait until to-morrow to see if Jem comes back with any information."

"It is very important," said the Chief, "that we should take that man. It is he who has kept the game going more than any other. His energy and honesty, and the hold he has upon the chapel-going work-men, keep many in the conspiracy who would otherwise leave it. I should be sorry to see him hanged, but it would be a good thing to get him out of the country for life."

"Well, Sir, you may depend upon John Green doing his best."

"That I am quite sure of," said the Chief kindly. "I have already written to the Government highly praising your skill and daring in the capture of the delegates and soldier."

Green determined to make one more attempt to get information in the town. Jem had told him all the particulars of his combat with Clogs, and knowing that musical genius well by sight, from the opportunity he had had of witnessing his performances by the hour together, and having learnt from Jem where he lived and where he worked, he prepared to throw himself in Clogs' way.

He made himself up as a costermonger, and trundling his wheelbarrow full of apples before him, planted it and himself at the edge of the footway of the street along which he knew that Clogs would pass to his dinner.

Shouting out " Apples, three a penny," at intervals, he anxiously waited for the dinner-hour.

The big gates of the mill were thrown open at twelve to the second, and like a swarm of bees out came the hands, some going in one direction others in another, until the mass had spread out like a fan, and individual members could be distinguished.

He at once recognized Clogs, for that youth immediately commenced airing his legs by a dance on the flagged footway, and having finished the performance t

the satisfaction of an admiring audience
he walked towards Green and his barrow.

"Three a penny, apples," shouted Green.
"Apples, three a penny; here, lads, put down
your coppers."

As Clogs approached, Green held in the
palm of his left hand three very fine rosy-
cheeked apples.

"Here, my lad; thou won't soon again
see the likes."

Clogs stopped and laid down the penny.

"Taste 'em," said Green, "and if thou
don't like 'em, I'll give thee others."

Clogs thereupon bit one, and, expressing
his satisfaction, Green said, in a spirit of
generosity,—

"Thou art a good lad for saying what's
only reet about the apples; here's one over
for thee," and then, looking intently at
him, said, "be thy name Clogs?"

"Yoi," said Jem.

"I thowt so," said Green, "for I heered

thy clogs going just now. Thou know'st my lad Jem, and pretty well too I reckon, he had a bout with thee in Wellgate-street."

Clogs was not well pleased at the reminiscence, but it had the effect Green desired, for Clogs forgot his dinner and stood talking and eating his apples the while.

"Jem told me," said Green, "that he'd seen thee standing in Wellgate-street when he came from the factory to breakfast, and on his way back, and again at dinner-time, both ways, and thou pushed him into the street, and he made up his mind to have it out with thee. What wast thou wer't staying for?"

"Staying for," said Clogs, "why to look about me."

"Here's another apple;" said Green. "Jem said thou fowt well. Dost thou know anybody in Wellgate-court? There's a chap in that court owes me for a barrowful of apples, and won't pay. He's a chapel-goer, and goes about praying with a man he calls Dick Basford—dost thou know him?"

" Noa," said Clogs, imperturbably.

" I think thou must," said Green, " and if I could only speak to Basford he might make him pay, as it do'ant look nice to go about praying, and owing for apples at the same time. Here's another apple for thee."

Jem received it, put it into his pocket, and to Green's great astonishment walked off without saying a word.

The native trustworthiness of the Lancashire boy was more than a match for the detective's cunning.

CHAPTER VII.

THE departure of Mr. Henry and Lawrie left a great blank in the household at the Close. The clear rolling voice of Mr. Henry, indicating health, strength, and happiness in old age, and the ringing childish laughter of little Lawrie lighted up the house and left dulness out of the question. Then was not Mr. Henry so open-handed, had he not dispensed "largesse" with liberality, was not Lawrie the pet of the house ?

His brothers were much older than himself—the elder by eight years, the other by six, so that they were in that crysalis state when they had neither the privileges of men nor the immunities of children. The two girls immediately above him in age were, as girls usually are, especially if the oldest child of the family be a girl, quiet and sedate, and the youngest was as a "baby," and a girl into the bargain, a thing to be played with, not to play.

So Master Lawrie had pretty nearly his own way in the matter of that which at a Spanish Posada is charged as "rumpus and riot." Not that he was allowed to carry on his pranks until he became, as a spoilt boy will become, a nuisance in the house, but his happy play and merry laugh were not checked by the harshness of an ignorant nurse, or the would-be genteel stiffness of a governess. His boyhood's boisterousness was tempered by a good mother's gentle restraint.

His old nurse missed him sadly. Her pockets, which in extent of accommodation more nearly resembled a sack than anything in the pocket line, were considered

the proper and fitting receptacle for all
Lawrie's toys, when, taking up first one
and then the other, he got tired of them,
and desired to deposit them in a place
of safety. Consequently, as the day drew
towards a close, nurse's increased width
of person became a matter of observa-
tion, and often did Mrs. Robert laugh
when nurse, almost stopped in her work
by the accumulation, had to unload a
most miscellaneous collection.

Mr. Robert himself, though somewhat
unbending with his children, liked to hear
Lawrie's innocent rattle when he came
home in the evening after the long labour
of the day, and missed his merry face when
he bargained with his nurse that she must
let him ride on her back up-stairs to
bed.

Mr. Henry had promised that he would
write to Mrs. Robert on the third day of
their arrival at Whicham, and say whether

he was content, and whether he was in the way or not, for she feared that, kind as Mr. Henry's intentions were, his bachelor arrangements might be inconsistent with the care of a child so young, and that, after a day or two, the trouble would become irksome, and she felt anxious to receive the promised letter, resolving in her own mind that if, on receipt of it, the slightest indication that Lawrie's visit disarranged the little establishment at Whicham she would go over over at once and fetch him. On the 4th day the postman brought the promised missive written in large well-formed letters, as was the custom of the last century. Mrs. Robert, with trembling hand, opened it and read as follows.

" Whicham, Sept. 3, A.D. 1819.

" My Dear Cousin Mrs. Robert.

" If I could express to you in appropriate terms the high appreciation in which I hold the affectionate and hospitable reception accorded to me by you and your most worthy and excellent husband, it would be with a pen of gold on tablet of silver. As I write this I respectfully kiss your hand through the medium of the post, and thank you from the innermost recesses of my heart. I look upon my cousin as the most fortunate of men in possessing a wife in whom are united all the beauties and virtues of her sex. I pray you, my dear Madam, to present to him my very kind regards and assurances that I shall ever be his affectionate and devoted relative.

" I am delighted to say that Master Lawrie has entered upon a country life with great enthusiasm. His advance in agricultural knowledge within two days has been astounding; he has rooted up the roses and planted the weeds in my garden to my great satisfaction. I beg pardon, my dear Madam, I mean that he has rooted up the weeds and planted the roses.

"I did myself the honour of calling on Mrs. Smyley. I regret to say that her reception was not very gracious, and she was pleased to allow me to take six copies of Dr. Smyley's hymns and six copies of his sermons, in return for which she was so good as to accept four pounds and ten shillings. One set I gave to Joseph, who has promised to learn them off by heart, and the others I shall present to the village school, if our Vicar will allow it.

"Lawrie sends his kind love at foot of this.

"I have the honour to be,

"My dear Madam,

"With the highest respect and esteem,

"Your devoted relative and servant,

"H. DE NOEL."

At the foot appeared the following in Lawrie's pot-hooks:—

"Lawrie very happy and sends love to Papa and Mamma."

Mrs. Lawrie kissed her boy's handwriting and felt quite at ease about him.

The fortnight which Mr. Henry had spent at the Close had been an exciting time for Mrs. Robert. At the end of it the reaction set in. Her husband noticed with intense anxiety that her cheeks got thinner and thinner, and that there was a cold moisture about the palm of her hand. The possibility of her being taken from him became daily more apparent.

The doctor did all he could to assuage his anxiety, but his good-natured efforts were unavailing. The proofs were too evident.

Mr. Robert thought that country air might restore his wife's health, and give her strength to go through the trial that awaited her—an addition to their family.

He bought an old-fashioned country house about five miles from Lumechester in the direction of Cheshire, with about eight acres of land attached to it, and there he determined to remove his wife so soon as the upholsterer could fit it for their reception.

By dint of coercion, persuasion, and a little bribery, he managed this in a few days, and the change evidently had a beneficial effect on Mrs. Robert.

A large square entrance-hall formed a reservoir for the pure air from the gardens and spread it through the house. The rooms were convenient with an air of comfort. A pure rippling stream ran through the grounds, enlarged at one part into a moderate-sized lake, upon which there was a small boat. The timber was very fine ; one old yew tree standing in the centre of the grass plot at the back of the house was an especial favourite of Mr. and Mrs. Robert.

There were good stables, coach-house, and other outhouses, and a well-stocked greenhouse, the choice plants in which had been purchased with the house.

It was a remarkably fine autumn, and as
Mrs. Robert sat on the garden seat under
the yew tree, she watched the " Indian summer" ripening to its close.

Reader, have you ever been amongst
the Catskill Mountains or the White
Mountains in the " Indian summer," as it
is called in America. If you have not, it is
a treat which alone is worth the crossing
of the Atlantic.

Place yourself on the little plateau in
the midst of the Catskills, where stands
the Mountain House Hotel, on a fine day
at the end of September or beginning of
October, and gaze down upon the valley
of the Hudson, lying some 3000 feet below
you—the river itself looking like a streak
of silver—this is the point to which old
Leather Stockings, one of Fennimore
Cooper's worthies, betook himself when he
wished to see " all creation. " You will
behold a glorious landscape, radiant in

brilliant hues, stretching to the foot of the Alleghany Mountains, some 80 miles off. The leaves have cast their monotonous green, and each tree vies with its neighbour in putting on its coat of many colours.

Or go to the White Mountains at the like time of the year, and standing at the summit of Mount Washington, over 6,000 feet high, look down on the landscape lying at your feet. The Indian summer in all its beauty—mountain and valley alike dressed in the colours of the rainbow.

We confess to having been sentimental the night we slept at the "Tip-top and Summit House," on the occasion of our visit to Mount Washington, and wrote in the visitor's book the following lines:—

> Imperial Mount!
> Aye is thy hoary head
> With wreath entwined,
> Like him who slumbers with the illustrious
> dead.

The cold winds call
In solemn accents from each clefted side,
  And bid thy sons
Behold fit emblem of their country's pride.

  Unmoved as he,
When slaughtered heroes round him fell,
  Do thou look down
On meaner mountain, rock, and dell.

  And when this globe
Dissolves with nature's mightiest throe,
  Be thou the last
To bow thy head in that great woe.

Mrs. Robert had her own misgivings about herself. She felt that the benefit she had received from change of air was but temporary, and she could not disguise the fact from herself that the trial before her would severely test all the strength she had left, and she trembled at the thought of leaving her dear children motherless.

Often when her husband came home in the evening to "The Yews," the name of their country house, he found her eyes red with weeping, her face full of anxiety; but she always attributed this to weakness, and said that he must not mind it, and that she would soon be better, and did all she could to prevent his getting low about her, and chatted with him until bed time, and the next morning put on a happy look, that he might not go forth to his struggles with the world with a load of anxiety on his mind.

One day she said to him that she thought it would be a great comfort to her if her only brother, she never had a sister, would come and stay a short time with her.

Mr. Robert most cordially gave his consent.

Having no loving brother or sisters, he had upon his marriage taken to his wife's brother with the same affection as if the two were brothers by blood, and in speaking to each other, and in their correspondence, they always addressed

each other as " brother," and the most
perfect confidence existed between them.

The Rev. Erasmus Godwin, that was the
name of Mrs. Robert's brother, was born
in Ireland, where he lived with his parents until about six years old, when he
came to England with them, and after some
years spent at school became a student at
the Independent College which had been
founded by the religionists of that name
for the education of their future ministers.

It was conducted in a liberal spirit as
regarded education, and in a conservative
spirit as regarded the status of the students. The arrangements were to a great
extent in imitation of the Universities of
Oxford and Cambridge; the students were
resident, the education was chiefly classical
and doctrinal, the expenses not inconsiderable, and a gentlemanly tone was incul-
cated.

We have in our mind, as we write, the

god-like form of one of the noblest beings
that ever preached the gospel of Christ to
man. We think we hear even now the
soul-stirring appeals which flew, as if in-
spired from on high, from those eloquent
lips. He had been a student at the college of which we speak.

Mr. Goodwin was a worthy representative
of the class of ministers it produced. A
fine head and forehead surmounted a face
of most benignant expression, a true index
of the character of the man. A kind
voice and winning manner put everyone
who was brought into contact with him
fully at ease. He married early a young
lady of good family and fair fortune, and
a most happy marriage it proved.

Shortly afterwards he received an invitation to become the pastor of the Independent congregation at Severnworth in
Shropshire.

It was in those days when Dissent was

looked upon as a vulgar thing, and its
ministers as low people unfit to associate
with the clergy of the Church of England;
and it was not a little to the credit of the
young pastor that, before he had been long
in the town, he had established friendly
relations with most of the clergy, and retained their good opinion to the day of
his death, though he never flinched from
advocating the doctrines and the civil and
religious rights of the members of his own
creed.

The chapel had been erected before his
time.

The town was divided into " upper "
and " lower, " the former standing at a
great height above the latter—some 150
feet or so perpendicular—and a great contention had arisen between the " Independents " residing in the former and those
in the latter as to the site for the chapel.
To such an extent was it carried that

there was considerable danger of a split in the congregation, and that each party would erect a chapel for themselves. The schism was at last healed by a site being secured half way between the "upper" and the "lower" town. It was the plateau of a projecting rock, with just sufficient space for the erection of a chapel of moderate size and a minister's residence. The approach to it was by steps cut in the solid rock, being, in fact, the ancient approach from the lower to the higher town.

In the chapel erected on this neutral ground, thrice every Sunday, and once each Wednesday, did Mr. Godwin exercise his ministrations, besides being during the week exemplary in his attendance upon the members of his congregation who from any cause required his services. His stipend, derived entirely from pew rents, was very small; indeed it was doubtful whether, deducting his charitable gifts to needy members of his congregation, he derived any pecuniary benefit from his appointment. His guileless nature made him listen to every appeal, and it was said that had it not been for the superior shrewdness of his wife, his income would have suffered still more.

A family of three children induced him to think of taking pupils, a step in which his wife fully concurred. He accordingly left the residence attached to the chapel, and became tenant of an ancient mansion in the lower town, which had been the family residence of the great squire who owned nearly all Severnworth and a large estate in land adjacent.

It was said to have been the house in which Cromwell and his associates met and decided on the death of Charles I. Sevenworth Castle, holding a commanding position in the upper town, had been bombarded by Cromwell and only the ruins remained.

There was a large banqueting chamber, one end of which opened into the private apartments of the family, and the other, by a broad oak staircase, led to those occupied by the servitors. An old oil painting of Charles I. on horseback formed a screen to the massive oak door which led from the banqueting-hall to the entrance gate. A yard, surrounded by a high wall, which in former days had been a drill ground for military vassals, was turned into a play-ground, and on the further side from the house a lofty capacious school room had been erected ; old stables and a coach-house stood on another side. A large, well laid out garden, with a sunk fence at the end, extended from the drawing-room windows, and beyond that was an orchard of productive fruit trees, and again beyond that a plantation rising considerably until it gained the level of the "Mall," a common where cricket and football were played.

Such was the residence of the Rev. Erasmus Godwin, and a happier abode could not well be imagined. His wife was an excellent manager, and consequently the *cuisine* was excellent, and the comfort of the pupils well caied for, so that she was always called by them " Mother," and if she ventured amongst them in the playground she was as much mobbed as ever was a royal personage by an English crowd.

The scenery of Severnworth was scarcely surpassed by any part of England. The Severn ran through the lower town, and formed a beautiful feature in the view from the upper town.

The noble park of the squire, now let to wealth gained by successful manufacture, was renowned for its extent, its variety of hill and valley, its fine timber, and splendid views.

If the Rev. Erasmus Godwin had a competitor in attracting the attention of his

congregation, it was the magnificent view
which, on a fine day in summer, could be
seen through the chapel doors when left
open to admit the balmy air.

CHAPTER VIII.

GREEN, whose feelings were much hurt by Clogs' ingratitude, was put into better mood by the information gained by Jem, who made his appearance at the office next morning, having reached Lumechester by the coach overnight. ·

Green told him of his attempt to worm out information from Clogs, and, when he got to the end of his story, Jem laughed heartily at the way in which he had been "done," and said he didn't think Clogs was half so sharp, and that he thought all the better of him for it, and that he would take an early opportunity of teach-ing him to fight on his toes, for he never would do any good so long as he fought flat-footed.

Green did not quite like Jem laughing at his discomfiture, and he was quite put out when the latter said that the master of the " Nancy " had told a brother bargee on the dock wharf how he had done the " runner " the night before, and that he had " swallowed it all like a child." Green could not help vowing that he would never rest till he had had the bargee " up " for poaching, for he'd be dashed if he'd be " sold for nothing."

They then laid their heads together - as to what was best to be done.

At last they settled that they should go to Drawbridge, but not together, Jem in his normal state of a factory boy out of work, and Green as a farm-labourer with a horse for sale.

The former was seen next morning walking briskly towards Drawbridge, his little bundle slung by a stick over his back.

Soon afterwards a farm-labourer apparently passed along the same road, riding a cart-horse, with only an old horse-cloth for a saddle and a rope for a bridle, and his tail tied up with gaudy ribbons. In rather over two hours they reached Drawbridge.

Green turned into the yard of an inn, and put his horse into the stable, and then sat down in the tap to a pint of ale and a pipe. Jem sat down on a door-step, near a large factory, looking pale and exhausted.

Shortly the hands came streaming out for dinner. They seemed to understand what he was, and though they · gave a look of pity they all passed on, except a lad rather older than Jem, who, looking at him for a moment, said, in a dialect different to the Lancashire,—

" What's the matter ? Out of work."

Jem replied that he was, and that he

had walked all the way from Lumechester that morning in hopes of getting some.

Jem noticed that his clothes were better kept, and his linen cleaner than was usual with factory hands ; and instead of leading him on, as at first he felt inclined to do, until he gave him an opportunity of having a " set to " with him—a thing which, as he had never been to Drawbridge before, he felt obligatory upon him—he returned an answer as if grateful to the questioner.

" Well, lad," said the latter, " I'm going to my dinner, and if you like you can come and have a bit."

Jem, quite willing, got up and walked with his newly-made friend.

As females were, equally with men, employed in the mills, the home of a factory hand was usually much neglected. The house-work was generally left to be done by some sickly member of the family unable to work, or by some old woman who, for a mere trifle, would put on the kettle and cook in her clumsy way the uninviting-looking bit of meat, or bacon and potatoes, for the family dinner.

Perhaps on a Saturday some little cleaning might be done to house and person; but, as a rule, the cottage had a dirty, neglected look, corresponding to the unwashed appearance of the inmates.

Jem's home was scarcely better than the average; though, since he had had to do with police matters he had paid more attention to his person, but not so as to detract from his appearance as a factory boy.

He was surprised, therefore, when on turning into a street on the other side of which there was a space with some struggling grass, interspersed here and there with decaying cabbage leaves and pieces of broken brick and earthenware, his companion entered a cottage which bore a strong contrast to the others in the row, and told him to come in.

On the sills of the front windows, both upper and lower, were ranged geraniums and fuschias in red-coloured flower-pots ; the windows themselves were clean and were half-concealed by nice white blinds with red cords and tassels.

On entering, Jem saw to his surprise that the room was well carpeted, and furnished with a polished table, chairs, and couch. A little bookcase, filled with books, stood in one corner; a nice clock ticked cheerily from the mantel-piece, and a neat paper ornament was spread over the grate, and fell on the fender and fireirons.

A canary warbled its notes from a cage hanging before the window.

"That's Stephe," said a girl's voice from the kitchen, which opened into the parlour, and immediately a girl of between fifteen and sixteen bounded into the room, and, seeing a stranger, suddenly stopped.

Her brother said, "This is a poor factory boy, Lilian, out of work. I found him seated, tired and hungry, on a step, and I've brought him home with me to have some of our dinner."

The girl looked at Jem as if she pitied him from her heart, and said, "Oh, yes; we shall be so glad. Dinner will be on the table in a minute."

Jem thought he had never seen such a being in his life before. She had fair hair, dark eyes, and a rosy complexion.

Her features were good. Her figure was tall and well-formed.

He stood in a kind of trance, until Stephen, putting his hand on his shoulder, said, "Come in here," and led the way into the kitchen, where Stephen's mother was putting the meal on the table.

Mrs. Bowthrop (that was her name) was

the widow of an under-bailiff in Sussex, and, during her husband's life, had enjoyed that plain but substantial comfort which a man in his position is usually blest with. But about four years before the time of which we are writing, he had died suddenly, leaving his wife and two children unprovided for. She struggled for about a year to preserve her position, and then, finding her efforts unavailing, she sold her furniture, and with the proceeds, and a sum which she received from the benefit society to which her husband belonged, she determined to go to Lancashire where, from all accounts, fabulous wages were made by the workpeople, and she thought her boy could obtain constant employment.

Armed with a letter from the vicar of the parish, she made her way by the stage-waggon with her two children to Drawbridge, where she had a cousin residing.

Her slender means were increased by a small weekly allowance from the employer of her late husband, a wealthy farmer, who promised to continue it until her son was old enough to earn wages sufficient to make her independent of it. She could not dispense with the comfort of a decent home, and she therefore furnished her cottage as well as her means would afford, and kept up her old habits of cleanliness and order, and impressed them on her children.

Still she could not quite reconcile herself to the change from the pure air of Sussex, and its health-giving downs, to a life in one of the " Sheeres," as she called them, which she had always been taught to regard as foreign parts, and the inhabitants thereof as akin to savages.

It was true her boy was getting on well. His intelligence and civility, coupled with strict punctuality at the mill and a kind of bearing which told of good bringing-up, had brought him the favourable notice of the overlooker, who had spoken well of him to the owner, and he had been raised above the ordinary position of boys of his age, with a corresponding increase of wages, and was looking forward to becoming an overlooker.

Only one hour was allowed at the mill for dinner, including going and returning, so that Jem had but little time to indulge in admiration of Lilian.

He made scarcely any dinner, for every word she spoke was a feast of itself for him, and when Stephen rose from the table he said,

"You've made a poor dinner, boy. I fear your coming here has done you little good."

Jem thought otherwise. "Done me no good," he exclaimed to himself; "hasn't it given me another life, a new world?"

He said, "Thank you kindly" to Mrs.

Howthrop, not daring to look at Lilian even, and left with Stephen.

The latter gave Jem his hand, and said he hoped that he would soon get work, and left him.

Jem stood for a moment to collect his thoughts; and then, recollecting that it was an hour since he arrived, and that he ought to have seen Green half-an-hour before at the inn, he hurried off there.

He went into the yard and gently opening the tap-room door, which was on the swing, put in his head and touched his cap, saying, in a piteous tone,

" Coppers for a poor factory lad, out o' work ? "

Green threw him a penny, and said, "Thou looks starved enough. There's a penny for thee ? "

That was the agreed on signal if Green had got information, and there was no further occasion to stay at the inn. Jem took up the penny, saying, "Thank thee," and left the yard; waiting, however, outside to see which way Green went.

The hour which Green had devoted to refreshment, for he had had something substantial in addition to the pint of ale and pipe, had been well employed. He had drawn the landlord into conversation, and got him on to the subject of the late monster meeting at Lumechester. That worthy, who leased his house from a landlord of decidedly Tory principles, was loud in his denunciations of it, and on Green bringing in cunningly the name of Basford, he said,

" Basford! Richard Basford! Aye, to be sure ; he's a Methody and lives here. He goes about praying and speechifying ; and now you speak about him, Bell, the butcher— Job Bell I mean—was here last night, and was saying that his horse were lame with going to near Crosdale. He did curse the

road, and said that Basford's wife had gone
with him. She was on her way to some
place or other."

"And is Bell's horse very lame;" asked
Green.

"Well, he said he were," replied the
landlord.

"May-be my horse in the stables will fit
him," said Green. "Whereabouts does he
live?"

The landlord directed him, and in
another minute or two Green was mounted
on his horse on his way to Bell's shop.

Jem sauntered along, keeping Green
in view, until the latter turned down the
street in which Bell's shop was.

As Green rode up he saw Bell standing in his shop and gazing intently
on the carcases of some sheep that were
hanging up.

"Thou'st been a bad lot to me," he said,
loud enough for Green to hear. "I've

lamed old Dan over ye, and now yer hung up I don't think either the parson or squire will have owt to do wi' ye."

Green dismounted and addressed the butcher :—

" Mester Bell, I hear thou'st lamed thy horse. Here's a good un and cheap."

Bell looked at the animal and then at Green.

" Who's thy master," said Bell.

Green gave the name of a farmer half way between Lumechester and Drawbridge, and with shrewd daring added that the landlord of the inn where he was stopping knew him and his master well.

" But how did thy horse get lame," said Green.

" Why," replied Bell, " I went over to Crosdale for some sheep. There they are, dang'em ; and I never see such a road in my life, and onst or twice, if it hadn't been for Richard Basford's wife, who was wi' me—and a mighty strong woman she is—helping me to get the cart out of a hole, I never could ha' done it, and, at last, I got to Farmer Thompson's, two or three miles on this side of Crosdale, where the sheep were, and came back again another road some miles round."

"And was the woman wi' thee to help thee back again," said Green.

"No," replied Bell, "she got out when I got to Thompson's. She was going on. She was going to Crosdale, but did na say where besides."

Green gave a sigh of disappointment, and determined to go on to Crosdale that very day.

"What does thou think of the horse," said Green.

Bell examined him and asked what the price was.

"Forty pound," said Green, naming a price not likely to be given.

" Then," said Bell, " thou'd better find somebody else to buy him."

Green mounted his steed and departed, Jem following. As soon as they got fairly out of the town, Green stopped and beckoned to Jem to join him. He told the latter what information he had got, and that it was a long way to Crosdale, and asked him if he would be able to walk it if he gave him a ride now and then, and Jem said he could. So they continued their journey in that direction.

Jem saw Lilian's face on every brake; it looked at him from the depths of every stream; it danced before him on the lonely moor.

CHAPTER IX.

PEACEFUL and sleepy as St. Peter's in the Rocks was at all other times, there were three days in the year when sounds of revelry were heard within its boundaries. It was the "Festival of Saint Peter's;" it began on the first Tuesday in September.

The preparations for it,—so important was it in the eyes of the inhabitants of the Rocks—began, it might be said, on the first of January in every year, and the re-collection of it remained until the first of January in the succeeding year. It corresponded, in many respects, to the *fête patronale* of the rural districts of France.

Those of our readers who delight in the

scenery of *la belle France,* must have been present at one of these fêtes. Take any florestral village, and there, once each year, takes place the *fête patronale.*

The village belles have been preparing for it for weeks, and the young farmers have been dreaming of it and the beautiful peasant girls they will meet there, quite as long.

Are not the "communal" bound to make it worthy of the village and the patron saint.

The authorities enter upon the preparations with a due sense of their responsibilities. As to the site there is generally no trouble. It is some open glade in the forest. Close by is a rural restaurant, the proprietor of which contributes liberally to the expenses.

Little tent stalls rise like magic in a single night. The "go rounds" and "swings" spring as it were from the ground. The coloured lamps lit up by oil are pendant from every tree. A space is prepared for the dancers, and rural seats are placed for the elders.

The "Maire," who arrives in his carriage with his buxom wife and laughing daughters, and son in the uniform of some provincial *école polytechnique*, opens the ball with the wife of some well-to-do farmer in the parish, and his son and daughters, enjoying the fun amazingly, readily find partners. Jeannot, cap in hand and with a low bow, begs the honour of dancing with Jeannette, whereupon the latter refers him to her mother or other married relative, under whose wing she nestles with charming modesty, and having received the requisite consent, stands up, first adjusting her little white cap and party-coloured petticoat, the continuation whereof is a pair of stockings, daintily worked from a little above the ankles, and hiding themselves in a neat pair of high-heeled shoes, fastened with pretty bows of ribbon.

A matron circulates amongst the dancers, and exacts from each cavalier the moderate sum of one *sou* for each dance.

The dance ended, Jeannot conducts his partner, leaning on his arm, to the protection of the elderly party aforesaid, and taking off his cap and uttering many thanks for the honour conferred upon him, subsides into the crowd.

No vulgar " kiss in the ring," allowing rough-handed, half-drunken men to impress their indecent lips upon the cheeks of young girls, who for the moment cast off the delicacy of their sex, and tempt the rude embrace.

The eye of the gendarme glances over the festive scene, and singles out any offender against the rules of propriety, and whispers in his ear that such as he are not wanted there.

At nine the festivities close, and if Jeannot
has been so charmed with Jeannette that
he cannot sleep that night, he makes his
way with sheepish look to her father's
cottage the next morning, and confesses to
the undying flame which burns within his
bucolic breast. But all little wanderings
in the forest on the evening of the *fête*, un-
attended by a brother or other protector,
are considered in bad taste, to say the
least.

In much the same spirit, but tempered
by the religious tone of the community,
was the festival of St. Peter's held. It
was not only festive in character, but it
was utilitarian as well.

The mountaineers, shut out from the world
as much by their own desire as by the
rocks which reared their heads above them
and stood sentry at the entrance of the
village, felt the necessity of having the
opportunity once a year of exchanging

their wares for those of the outside world. The things in daily use could not last for ever, and the way to the towns was long and rough.

Ebenezer was not the man to overlook the advantage to the village of an annual festival, which, whilst it enlivened the little community, added no inconsiderable amount to its wealth. It was he who promoted, guided, and controlled this annual *fête*.

Many weeks before the time of holding it he called together the elders of the village, and arranged everything with them.

Nature had, fortunately for St. Peter's in the Rocks, provided unusually favourable opportunities for holding this annual festival. At the upper end of the village there was a rock which rose perpendicularly more than three hundred feet above the road. It went by the familiar name of the " Patriarch," and on its summit were the remains of Druidical temples. Between the road and the rock was a considerable space of green sward, and after crossing that was the entrance, which was wide and lofty, into the cavern.

On first entering the visitor stood astonished at its magnitude. The roof was eighty feet from the ground and studded with stalactites, which on being lighted up shone like stars in the firmament. It was, taking an average, about four hundred feet wide and six hundred feet long. Vast masses of rock overhung the sides.

The floor was of beautiful sand, as if the mighty ocean had once filled the cavern and left a memorial behind. The sand, the overhanging rocks, the stars, led one to imagine oneself in the deserts of Arabia.

At the further end was a cascade, which fell from a height of nearly fifty feet into a dark pool below, and from the force of the fall elongated itself into a lake about one hundred and fifty feet across, called by the classical name of Lake Lethe. Then it lost itself in an opening in the rocks, and reappeared at the point where it was received by the village conduit.

It was in this cavern that the festival was held.

On its approach Ebenezer did all he could to ensure success. Invitations were issued to the leading tradesmen of the neighbouring towns to send specimens of their best wares for sale—Ebenezer would have none but the best of their kind. He knew exactly what the people of the Rocks wanted, and made his requisitions accordingly.

The cave was marked out in sections, and on one side were the "foreign" and on the other the native products.

The staple manufacture of the valley, as

well as of St. Peter's, was woollen cloth, and
this was brought to great perfection.

That which was exhibited at the festival
was of the best kind, and merchants from
the large towns came to see what could
be effected by native skill as compared
with the looms of Belgium and other
countries.

The valley people and those of St. Peter's
vied with each other in producing cloth of
the finest material and most brilliant hues,
chiefly for the Italian and Spanish markets,
and as the long drapery hung in bright
and mixed colours on the stalls it produced
a brilliant effect.

The light from the entrance penetrated
but a short distance into the cavern.

Oil lamps of many-coloured transparent
paper gleamed from the crevices of the
rocks ; they were carried along the natural
galleries above them ; they lay almost hidden in the ground ; they peered through

the waters of the cascade, and cast their light on the lake.

In addition to all these the renters of the stalls had their own special illuminations and vied in producing a brilliant effect.

The female costume of the mountaineers was very picturesque. Bonnets were not used, but a small white handworked lace cap fitted to the top of the head, and was fastened with a silver bodkin. A bodice of white or black lace was thrown over the shoulders and fastened at the waist. Petticoats of red blue or bright brown were usually worn. Home-knit stockings and laced-up boots completed the costume, which was at once useful and becoming.

The men wore a jacket unbuttoned at the neck, with a loose, bright-coloured silk handkerchief over the shirt collar; a belt, knee breeches, blue or gray stockings, strong laced-up boots, and a felt hat not unlike the modern wide-awake.

When the cavern was fairly filled with people, it looked like a village scene in an opera. A watchful eye was kept by Ebenezer and his associates upon those who entered, and if any suspicious-looking character presented himself, he was courteously informed that it was a private gathering, not open to every person indiscriminately.

For this particular festival great preparations had been made.

Ebenezer's two sons had promised to attend, accompanied by some of their comrades. They sailed from London in one of the fine schooners which plied between the Thames and Hull, and made their way on foot to St. Peter's, highly pleased with their journey, and much improved in condition.

We have before referred to the musical talent of the working classes of Lancashire.

Ebenezer, who had himself a taste for

music, secured some good voices from Crosdale and the neighbourhood for the performance of Locke's grand and weird-like strains in " Macbeth."

Mary Basford had thrown herself heart and soul into the preparations for the festival. Her nature was essentially impulsive, and she longed for some sphere in which to exercise her tendencies. She it was who with her husband's assistance and that of some of the villagers, who were experienced in such matters, arranged the lamps, marked out the spaces for the tents, fixed upon the retired nook for the fortune-teller, directed where the swings and roundabouts should stand, and generally put things in order.

Ebenezer was only too glad to have so efficient an assistant, and congratulated her husband on having so business-like a wife.

Richard Basford gladly succumbed to the superior tact and, in such matters, energy of his wife, and looked on highly pleased at what she did, and paid her, as she said, more compliments than he had done all the time they had been married.

The first Tuesday in September opened in brilliant sunshine, with a promise of fine weather.

The good people of Saint Peter's were early astir.   In almost every house preparation had been made to receive friends, and for those who had no house to go to Ebenezer had made arrangements for their accommodation.

On the conclusion of peace there had been a sale at Crosdale of Militia tents, and Ebenezer, feeling the want of accommodation at St. Peter's at festival times, had bought a considerable number of them for a mere trifle, and they had been arranged in rows on the green sward at some little distance from the entrance to the cavern, and fitted-up in a rough but clean way for the accommodation of visitors.

Amongst others who availed themselves of this convenience were the comrades of Saul and Seth Thorneycroft, Ebenezer's two sons. Two of the largest tents were assigned to the civil, well-conducted landlord of the inn in the valley, and there he dispensed refreshments.

The cavern was opened for admission at one o'clock, Ebenezer rightly considering that hour sufficiently early. The first proceeding on each day was to sing an appropriate hymn, in which the trained voices from the Crosdale district took the lead, and joined by the rest within the cave, sent forth a volume of sound which echoed from side to side and lost itself in the lofty roof.

CHAPTER X.

GREEN and Jem reached Crosdale late in the evening. They and the ribbon-decorated steed were thoroughly tired, and Green quite endorsed the opinion of Bell the butcher as to the road. They went to one of the taverns in the neighbourhood of the Market-place, where Green had no difficulty in obtaining accommodation for himself and horse, and, passing off Jem as a poor factory lad whom he had overtaken quite exhausted on the road, got the ostler to let him have a rough couch in his own cottage, and the latter, taking rather a liking to Jem from his knowledge of the noble science, which he accidentally discovered, was not unwilling to let Jem remain until he got some work.

Green had not the slightest clue to Mary Basford's route after she left Bell at Thompson's farm, and he set to work to find out something about her.

His pretended sale of the horse gave him an opportunity of dropping in at the different taverns in the town in search of a customer, and managing very adroitly to work the conversation in the right direction, ascertained that no person answering Mrs. Basford's description had been at any of them.

He then ascertained the different lodging houses in the town, and under one pretence or another called at each, except the one where Mrs. Basford had actually stayed, and that he passed over understanding that it was a house of indifferent reputation, and about the last place that a woman of Mrs. Basford's character would stop at.

At last he began to despair, and felt
that if he stayed in Crosdale much longer
he might himself become an object of
suspicion.

The landlord already began to joke him
about his want of success in the horse-dealing
line, and the ostler broadly declared that
if he stayed much longer his steed would
eat his head off.

Jem had done all in his power by
mixing among the factory boys to pick
up scraps of information, and, being out
of temper at his failure, had picked a
quarrel with a butcher's boy about his
own age and height, who had won some
renown with his fists, and the affair
came off in a field in the outskirts of the
town, the ostler at the inn backing Jem
and expressing his delight at his skill and
pluck.

When in the evening Green met Jem
by appointment and saw that his face show-

ed signs of punishment, he simply said " Hast thou lickened ? "

" Yoi," said Jem, and no further obser-vation was made by either of them on the subject.

Green had determined to return the next day to Lumechester, and mentioned this re-solve to Jem, who fully agreed in its ex-pediency, and it was arranged that each should prepare accordingly.

Green paid his bill at the tavern and found Jem the money to pay the ostler, but the latter refused to take anything from him, saying that he had taken long odds against Jem's winning, as the butcher boy looked so much the bigger lad of the two, and that he had pocketed a " fiver " by the result.

Green and Jem were actually on the road home when a sudden thought struck Green. He pulled up his horse and beck-oned to Jem, who always kept a hundred yards or so before or behind him, to join him.

"Jem," he said, " there's one lodging-house in Crosdale I haven't been at, and I didn't go because it bears a bad name; may be Mrs. Basford went there not knowing the kind of place it is, and as we are here why shouldn't I clear the thing up?"

Jem, in whose good sense and acuteness Green began to place much confidence, said he didn't see why he shouldn't have a try.

Green determined to return at once to Crosdale, but without Jem or the horse, and not to re-enter the town until dark.

They accordingly stopped at a roadside tavern about two miles from Crosdale, where he again palmed off Jem as the tired factory boy out of work, and pretending to have left something behind him at Crosdale, arranged with the landlord to give Jem a bed, and stable his horse for the night. A little before dusk he started off to Crosdale.

He entered the town as it became dark, and went direct to the house in the street leading off the main street where Mrs. Basford had stopped the night. He was at once promised a bed, for he appeared to be of the same class as the usual frequenters of the house, and was shewn into the room on the ground floor where Mrs. Basford had taken her supper.

Taking a pipe and putting down the money for a quart of ale, which the landlord sent for, he asked the latter if he would join him, as he felt lonely by himself.

The landlord, nothing loth, took a chair, and, after some talk about the weather and the crops, Green began to feel his way.

"Did the landlord," he enquired, "know how horses went at the last fair; for he had one that he wanted to sell, but before bringing it to Crosdale he should like to know something about prices." And this led to some discussion about its age, height, etc., and the information which Miles the landlord could give him from overhearing the conversation of the horsedealers who came to his house being apparently satisfactory to Green, he said that he should bring the horse the next fair day, and take up his quarters at the house, adding that if in the meantime Miles could find him a purchaser he would give him a pound for himself, an offer which at once established Green in Miles' good graces.

At this point Miles' wife opened the door a little, and said, "Miles, thou art wanted."

Miles said, turning to Green, "By your leave," and left the room and pulled the door to after him ; but, the clasp not catching, it immediately opened slightly, and Green could hear, though the conversation in the passage was in a low tone, and the voices were gruff, that it was something about a woman, and distinctly heard the question asked, " Has she been here since ?" Here Mrs. Miles joined in, speaking low, and said, " Not likely—she's a decent married woman, and I hope thou left her safe at foot o'th' valley."

The door was just enough open to allow Green, who had stepped on tiptoe to the door, to see that there were two thickset men, looking like graziers, in the passage, talking to Miles and his wife.

On hearing what the latter said, they gave a coarse laugh, and one said, " D—— her, she ought to be at foot of a pit."

Then they hinted that there had been a bit of a disturbance, and asked if any one had been there asking questions, and on being told there had not, they enquired who was in the house, and learning that there was only a farm labourer, who wanted to sell a horse, they said they would stay all night.

Green was back on his chair instantly, for the next moment they pushed open the door, and drawing chairs near the table sat down, and one of them, taking some silver from his pocket, told Miles to fetch a bottle of rum, and bring hot water and pipes.

Green, as being there first, said " Good evening, " to which they both replied by a nod and a grunt.

Green in his time had met with some bad-looking fellows, but he thought he had never seen two such ruffians before, and he inwardly calculated how he should " tackle " two men so powerful and determined.

The rum and its accessories were brought by Miles, and they insisted upon his sitting down and joining them.

They filled their own tumblers and his

half full of rum, adding only so much water as made the mixture warm, and after some general conversation, Miles, in thieves' jargon, which Green understood, asked them about the woman whom they had taken away in their cart to the foot of the valley.

With many oaths, and in thieves' jargon also, the men gave an account of the affair, and on describing how they had been felled to the ground and left insensible, their faces assumed the look of demons.

They then told how they had followed up in their cart, and had been ordered out of the valley.

During this recital they frequently looked askance at Green, who, however, maintained the innocent look of a farm labourer, which they felt assured he was.

Courageous as he was, Green did not like the idea of going to bed with two such men in the house. He must start for the valley the next day, and sleep was necessary for him, and that he felt he could not have—at all events not sound sleep—if there was a chance of those men entering his room to see the inside of *his* purse, in which he had a considerable sum of money. But he saw no alternative. It was then ten o'clock, and were he to leave it would create suspicion, and they might follow him and set upon him in a lonely part of the road.

Then again the landlord at the road side inn might be in bed and refuse to let him in under any pretence, and if he did admit him there might not be a vacant bed.

So he determined to stay and run all chances.

Another bottle of rum was ordered and the men pressed Green to join them, but he said that he had had some ale and never drank spirits.

Thereupon they insisted upon Mrs. Miles coming in and joining them, and one of them made her a powerful glass of rum and water.

Green asked her what time it was, and she answering " Ten o'clock," he rose, and saying " Good night," asked Miles for his bedroom, which the latter, holding a rusty candlestick, in which there was the half of a dip candle, showed him down a long, narrow passage, on each side of which were bed-room doors, and opened the last door on the right.

He did not hear Miles's steps leave the door for some minutes, and felt that he was being watched from some chink or hole in the door, but he sat down on the edge of the bed and, yawning loud, said,—

" I'm blest if I'm not tired," and then began whistling, all the while keeping an attentive ear for Miles's departing footsteps, and at last hearing them, he took the candle and looked carefully round the room.

He did not care so long as he was not attacked in sleep, for he not only had his truncheon concealed beneath his smock frock, but he had the long dagger which he had taken from the soldier.

He examined the door, and finding that there was no lock or bolt, but only a latch, he thrust his penknife between the lift and the guard. Then he removed the washstand from the other end of the room, and placed it, jug, basin, and all against the door. Then putting his truncheon and dagger unsheathed on the chair at his bed-head, he resolved to go to sleep come what might.

He had been asleep about three hours when he heard dull, heavy footsteps, as if those of men in stocking-feet coming slowly down the passage.

Jumping in an instant noiselessly out of bed, and taking his trusty truncheon in his right hand and the dagger in his left, he stood near the hinges of the door, which opened from the wall, ready for anything.

Nearer the steps came, and though the colour left Green's cheek, as is usually the case with determined men, not for an instant did he feel fear.

The steps approached, until they stopped opposite his door.

Green's nerves were now strung up to their highest tension, for the next moment' he expected the door and the barricade to be dashed in.

To his great relief the opposite door was opened and then closed ; still that was not sufficient to remove all apprehension, and he remained on guard at the door.

In about ten minutes the opposite door was again opened and closed, and the muffled footsteps disappeared down the passage and Green got into bed again and fell asleep.

In the morning he rose early, and after taking an uninviting breakfast he asked for his bill.

Miles, laying it on the table, said, "I trust thou did'st not hear any disturbance last night. Those men made my wife and me both drunk, and they had to carry her to bed. I fell asleep downstairs, and there they left me."

Green laughed, and replied that he had heard them, but they only kept him awake for a minute or two.

There was no question in Green's mind but that Mrs. Basford was the woman that had been ill-treated by the ruffians, and that her husband, having worked in a north-easterly direction from Whicham, had by accident been able to rescue her from their hands, and that when he got to Evendale he should hear more about them.

He quickly walked the two miles to the inn where he had left Jem and the horse, and getting out the horse and telling Jem to follow, he hurried through Crosdale on the road to the valley.

He reached there in the afternoon, Jem taking his turn on horseback, and going into the inn took his horse into the stable.

He found the little town quite forsaken. The landlord was not in nor were his wife or any of his children. The only person left in charge was a help in the stables, a lad about the age of Jem, and as the latter had him all to himself he soon pumpéd out of him all about Basford and his wife, and which route they took after taking refreshment at the inn, and the scene which occurred with the ruffians. And all this corroborated Green's opinion that at last he was on the right track.

He was at no loss to discover the cause of the absence of the landlord and his family ; for large placards, announcing the festival and the various things to be seen there, were posted on the walls of the inn, and at several places in the small town.

The advertisement was worded in terms free from all exaggeration and was headed " D. V."

CHAPTER XI.

LAKE LETHE.

AFTER the opening hymn had been sung in the Patriarch's Cave the festival began. There were over 1,000 persons present. The renters of stalls in a quiet way, free from touting or pressure, explained the character of their wares. No one was allowed to call out to the passers-by, urging them to purchase.

Ephraim Norman carried the self-taught artist in his strong arms to the spot where it was arranged that he should have his table placed to exhibit his drawings of the indigenous plants of the district. Rachel stood by his side and was saleswoman, and by her winning smile readily gained customers for her husband's productions.

Mary Basford had been selected to repre-

sent the gipsy fortune-teller; her black
hair and dark features, as well as her shrewd
wit, fitting her for the post, and got up
in red cloak and gipsy bonnet, and seated
in a dim recess of the rocks, she looked
and acted the character admirably.

Richard Basford was stationed on the
shore of Lake Lethe, and dispensed from
an antique goblet a drink of the waters
of the lake.

Close to where he stood there was a
large board affixed to the rock, on which
the following lines were inscribed in clear
characters :—

> Boyhood, standing on this brink,
> Wait a moment ere thou drink!
>   Think of every lispéd prayer
>   Wafted on the evening air,
>   Taught by mothers' lips so true,
>   Eyes of fondness bent on you—
>   Hast thou caused that mother grief,
>   And would from sorrow seek relief?
> Then raise dark Lethe's cup and drink,
> And never of that grief you'll think!

Girlhood, standing on this brink,
List a moment ere thou drink!
   Think of fathers' beaming smiles
   Laughing at thy infant toils,
    To climb on shoulder or on knee,
    Crowning success by kissing thee—
    Hast thou aught done thou would'st hide
    Lest it wound that father's pride?
Then raise dark Lethe's cup and drink,
And never of that fault you'll think!

Bride and bridegroom, on this brink
Pause a moment ere ye drink!
   Looking in each other's eyes
   Vowing that no earth, no skies,
    Ever gave to wedded pair
    Such deep rapture as ye share—
    Would ye that such bliss should be
    Swept away from memory?
Then raise dark Lethe's cup and drink
And never of that bliss ye'll think!

Aged couple, on this brink
Stay a moment ere ye drink!
   Have ye climbed the hill together,
   Sharing fair and gloomy weather,
    Holding up each other's hand
    As ye trod life's dangerous strand?
    If ye have not, let it be
    Banished from your memory—
Then raise dark Lethe's cup and drink
And never of the past ye'll think!

At three o'clock the assault at arms took place, Saul and Seth Thorneycroft being the leading actors. Including the two Thorneycrofts there were eight Guardsmen, all picked men.

The broad-sword exercise, sword and bayonet, and the feats of cutting a sheep in two and cleaving solid bars of iron were exhibited to perfection, and drew forth loud shouts of applause. Then followed boxing, wrestling, and throwing the hammer.

No one seemed more interested in these sports than Ebenezer himself. He had been a celebrated athlete, and took a pleasure in teaching his two sons to box, wrestle, and throw the hammer, and in these exercises they stood pre-eminent in their regiments.

At five o'clock Locke's music in " Macbeth " was given in costume in a part of the cave well adapted to the purpose, and as the vocalists were efficient it was a great treat to the mountaineers, who, like that class generally, were imbued with a great love of the wild and marvellous. The chaldron scene especially was a great treat to them.

From seven to nine Ebenezer and his coadjutors encouraged dancing, and parties were formed in different parts of the cave, and footed it to the music of a " valley" band, consisting of a flageolet, violin, and harp, aided by a triangle.

At nine a gong was sounded, and as soon as the cave could be cleared the large gates were drawn to, and Ebenezer himself locked them, and put the ponderous key into his pocket.

It was on the second day of the festival that a farm labourer entered the village, leading a horse, the tail of which had been newly decorated with many coloured ribbons, and his mane twisted and tied into knots with straw, and streamers of ribbon fell over his face.

Outside the cave a piece of ground, enclosed with wooden railings, had been set apart for such animals as were on sale— horses, asses, cattle, sheep, goats, and pigs were there ranged, and though not numerous there was a fair amount of dealing going on.

The man who led the decorated steed by a halter made divers inquiries as he passed up the village, from which it was evident that he was a stranger to the place, and was also unknown in Evendale, as none of the valley people spoke to him.

This would not have been a matter of surprise had he not been a labourer in appearance; but as all the men of that class were well known it attracted ob- servation.

Green made his way to the enclosure for the sale of animals, and fastened his horse to a rail.

Word had been passed to Ebenezer that

a "foreigner" had been seen passing up the village with a horse for sale, and had put it in into the enclosure.

Ebenezer at once came up to Green, and asked him where he came from and whose horse it was; to which he replied that he was servant to a farmer living half way between the valley and Crosdale, giving his name (which was not unknown to Ebenezer); but the latter said it was odd that the farmer should send his horse for sale to an out of the way place instead of to Crosdale, when Green replied that he had tried the last fair at Crosdale and' could not get his price, and hearing of the festival he thought he would try and sell there, and quite took away Ebenezer's suspicion, when he added with charming frankness that he didn't want "to handle th' money," and that if he sold, Ebenezer should hold the money until he could hear from his master.

No further objection was raised to Green's stay, and Ebenezer rather took himself to task for suspecting the man.

Green ticketed his horse with the price, a plan usually adopted there, and went into the cave.

Some little distance behind him walked in a pale-looking factory boy, but as he was young and had probably come from Crosdale no notice was taken of him.

Green showed such tokens of wonder and admiration as might be expected from a farm labourer seeing the brilliant sight for the first time.

He walked round the cave, and seeing a board up "to the gipsy," he went with others towards the table where Mrs. Basford sat.

"Mrs. Basford! as I'm alive," said Green to himself, "and her husband's not far off I'll be bound."

He continued his ramble, and came to

where Basford was engaged doling out the waters of the lake, receiving a small gratuity from each drinker.

He knew that, occupied as they were, he might safely calculate upon both remaining until the closing of the cave.

He then stationed himself close to the roped-off space where the athletic sports were to take place.

Green dearly loved all such pastimes. Being a Cumberland man he had been accustomed before he joined the police to wrestling on his native green, and had studied the "noble art," and he often attributed his successful encounters with daring characters to the confidence and self-reliance which he gained by those accomplishments.

The Guardsmen, who had been vociferously cheered the day before, were, with the exception of Saul and Seth Thorneycroft, who were as modest as they were brave, a little elated, and were disposed to give themselves airs as if despising the rustics around them,

The boxing began, and Green, who was so near the ropes that anything he said was heard by the soldiers, passed some comments on the performances of one or two of the number, not intending that they should be heard ; but they came almost involuntarily from his lips.

It was evident that two of the men were annoyed at his criticisms and turned angry looks towards him, which Green did not observe, though the bystanders did.

The boxing ended, the wrestling began. The sand was covered with good thick matting to break the falls, and the eight men wrestled a " main," the conquered leaving the ring, until Saul Thorneycroft and a young giant of about twenty-three were left opposed to each other, when after a severe struggle the young one was thrown a clean back fall.

This contest excited a keen interest in Green's mind, and he thought the young one might have won had he not made a mistake, and this opinion he expressed audibly.

The young Guardsman, smarting under his defeat, turned sharply round to Green, and said, "You have been expressing your opinion pretty freely about our boxing and wrestling. I don't fancy you would like to try a fall?"

"Yes," said Green, "I should."

The soldier looked at Saul Thorneycroft, as if to say, "Any objection?" on which Saul said coolly, "You have given the challenge and you can't as a Guardsman get out of it, although it does seem ridiculous to wrestle with a country pumpkin."

Green heard the reply, and if anything it gave him additional nerve.

"Wait a moment," he said to the soldier, and going out of the crowd told the factory boy to mind his clothes and he would give him some coppers.

Dexterously folding up unseen his truncheon and dagger in his smock-frock, he took off his waistcoat and shirt, leaving on his vest and fastening his trousers to his waist by his braces, and turning up his trousers to his calves, he entered the ring.

The event caused immense excitement in the cave, and Ebenezer at first was inclined to stop it peremptorily, but his sons pointing out that the Guardsman had challenged the countryman and could not back out of it, Ebenezer gave way, but warned all the lookers-on that they must not disturb order by too much demonstration.

The men grappled, and everyone expected that the superior size and youth of the Guardsman would decide the event at once, but, to their astonishment, after a struggle of about five minutes Green gave him "the lock," and threw him a clean back fall.

Notwithstanding Ebenezer's warning there was loud applause.

Green might then have left the ring, but his antagonist seemed so chagrined that he offered to wrestle the best of three falls, which was agreed to.

In the second "bout" Green was thrown after a short struggle and the excitement became intense.

In the third the struggle lasted about six minutes, when Green gave his man the "half buttock," and threw him a clean back fall.

This time the crowd could not be restrained, but cheered Green vociferously, and the result might have been to destroy the harmony of the meeting, had not the

young Guardsman generously held out his
hand to Green, and said that so good a
wrestler as he was had a right to comment
on the wrestling of others.

With the assistance of Jem, Green donned
his clothes, and became for the rest of the
evening an object of marked attention.

When the cavern was closed at nine
o'clock, Green kept Basford and his wife
in view until they ascended the ladders
at Ebenezer's house, and his keen eye
noticed the ladder lying by the door of
the gaol. He concluded that they were
the guests of Ebenezer, and looking at the
isolation of St. Peter's, the character of
the inhabitants, and the influence of Ebenezer over them, he felt that the arrest of
Basford there and then might cost him his
life, and that it would not be an easy task
even if all the police force of Lumechester
were to undertake it.

He therefore determined to let the festival end and the excitement subside before he made the attempt, and to remain quietly in the valley himself, leaving Jem on the watch at St. Peter's.

After shewing the latter Ebenezer's house, he told him to keep a watch upon those coming out and going in, and to make himself acquainted with the appearance of Basford and his wife, and explained where he would find them in the cavern next day, and saying that he might expect him on the second day from then, and that he must be on the look-out on the valley road until he saw him, he left him.

Jem had managed to make acquaintance with Ephraim Norman, and the latter asked him to stay at his house for a day or two, an offer which Jem thankfully accepted, and as they chatted the next morning over their breakfast, Jem was able to get a good deal of information about Ebenezer and his household.

On the third day of the festival Jem went to the Patriarch's Cave as soon as it was opened, and made himself well acquainted with the appearance of Basford, by having a drink of the water of Lake Lethe, and of his wife by having his fortune told.

He carefully studied the doings within the ring, was full of admiration of the music in " Macbeth," and managed to get a little village maiden to be his partner in a country dance ; but he thought she was not to be compared to Lilian, nor could he see any other girl at the festival " fit to be named on the same day."

He watched Ebenezer's house at the close of the day, and found that, besides Ebenezer and his two sons, Basford and his wife and two of the elders entered it, and that all remained except the two elders, who left in about an hour, and then the lower ladder was lifted up.

On the next day the visitors left St. Peter's. The stalls and fittings-up in the cave and the tents outside were removed, and St. Peter's began towards evening to assume its usual quiet look.

About mid-day, Ebenezer, with a large leathern satchel slung over his right shoulder and brought under the left arm, mounted his horse, and, accompanied by his two sons and their comrades on foot, took the direction of the valley.

Green saw them approaching the inn, and buried himself in the stable until they left in the direction of Crosdale, and rightly' conjectured that Ebenezer was going on business there which would keep him all night from home. Now was the opportunity he had longed for.

He went to a rope-walk in the valley, and purchased a long length of good, strong rope, and seeing accidentally a thick iron spike lying about the stables at the inn, which could be driven eighteen inches into the ground, and still leave the same length above, he borrowed it from the ostler, and with the spike in his hand, and the rope coiled over his right shoulder and under his left arm, he started for Saint Peter's.

He met Jem about a mile from the village, and sitting down in a field at some distance from the road side, he learnt from Jem about Ebenezer starting from home, and that he had heard Mrs. Basford say good-bye to him, and that she would have supper ready for him the next evening, and that Basford shook hands with him in the road and wished him a " pleasant journey," and that in the evening Basford drew up the lower ladder.

After a rest, which was very grateful to Green, they rose, and instead of keeping to the main road they turned up a footpath to the right, which Green thought would lead to the top of the rocks over Ebenezer's house.

He was right. On reaching the top they found a cleft in the rocks, and, descending it, they reached a point immediately above the house with a clear fall of only about twenty feet to the garden below.

There they left the rope and spike covered over with decayed leaves, and, returning by the footpath, went into the village, where Green pretended to search in the neighbourhood of the cave for a shoe which his horse had cast.

About midnight Basford was startled by a knock at his bedroom door, and a clear determined voice said,—

"Richard Basford, you are my prisoner —come out."

Basford, pale as the victim doomed to the guillotine, when the executioner opening his cell door exclaims, "L'heure est arrivée," stepped forward and was arrested.

CHAPTER XII.

MASTER Lawrie's days were all too short for him, his meals were useless interruptions, bed-time was lost time.

Early as Mattie rose she found her charge quite ready for the bath, but very impatient over the arrangement of the curls.

Mrs. Robert, with her usual forethought, took care that he should take with him a plain suit of clothes and strong shoes, for rough work in Mr. Henry's garden, and in Moore's farm-yard and fields, from which she knew it would be impossible to exclude him.

He took upon himself the care of a

brood of chickens, shewing more anxiety than the old hen herself.

He adopted a supernumerary young porker, one of a large litter, which, being the feeblest of the lot, was pushed aside at feeding time, and stood a good chance of starvation, and it was a sight to see Lawrie, assisted by Joseph, giving the little animal, which was kept separate and as clean as soap could make it, its morning and evening meals, through the medium of a teapot with an imitation teat at the end the spout. In return it formed quite an affection for Lawrie, and followed him about like a dog. Then there were the foal and calf to be petted.

Joseph was fond of birdcatching, and soon collected a miscellaneous assemblage, from the blackbird to the sparrow, which he kept in an outhouse, and they had to be attended to every morning, and water and food given them.

The only thing about the place which shewed spite to Lawrie was a little bantam cock, which resented his hens being driven about, and on one occasion flew at Lawrie's face and tried to peck out his eyes, and might have done him some injury if Mattie, who was always more or less on the look out for him, had not run to the rescue, and, seizing the offending bird, condemned him to the spit.

Often did she lose him for a short time, and generally found him fast asleep from fatigue on some new hay or a green bank, with the little porker by his side.

Milk, warm from the cow, innocent of any acquaintance with the relative of the iron tail, home-made bread, dishes daintily dressed by Mrs. Moore, and comprising venison from the Earl's, fish from the great Commoner's "mere," and game and fruit from others, put Master Lawrie in clover, and he thrived accordingly, and before the end of a fortnight might, from his bronzed complexion, have passed for a little gipsy.

The only drawback in his opinion was that his little sister was not with him to share his delight.

On the first Sunday after Lawrie's arrival he had to forego, to his great sorrow, the freedom of the week day.

Joseph himself was compelled to put on a face appropriate to the day.

Mattie took out the velvet dress and its belongings, which Lawrie declared were not half so nice as his week dress, and arrayed him therein, and told him that he was not to go near his favourites, whether quadruped or biped, until the next morning. And he gave her a kiss and took out the bright half-crown and gave it to her.

She at first declined to receive it, but Lawrie said that his mamma had told him to give it away if he liked, and this Joseph confirmed, and so she accepted it, and his generous spirit made her love him the more.

"The church-going bell" began its not very melodious notes, and warned Mr. Henry that they must prepare to go.

Joseph, who knew his duty, entered the library, and took under his arm Mr. Henry's ponderous Prayer-book and Bible. The latter was a "family Bible," and contained divers entries of births, deaths, and marriages in the De Noel family. It was of very ancient date, and fastened with big clasps, and the print was large and clear, and well adapted to Mr. Henry's great age. The Prayer-book was a match to the Bible.

Mr. Henry, taking Lawrie by the hand and followed by Joseph with the books under his arm, strode with stately steps to the church.

The parishioners were in the habit of assembling in the churchyard to await the arrival of the vicar, a man much beloved by his flock. He was gentle and kind and blameless in his life and conversation.

Mr. Henry loved to keep up the practice of showing honour to the vicar, and no one more respectfully raised his hat to him than did Mr. Henry, as the former passed through the lines formed by the congregation. On this occasion the worthy clergyman, who generally walked past into the church without recognizing any one, stopped as he came to Mr. Henry, and taking him affectionately by the hand, expressed his great delight to see him again after the dangers he had gone through, and, bending down, kissed Lawrie, whom he knew to be his godson.

Then with the rest of the congregation Mr. Henry entered the church, and holding Lawrie's hand proceeded to his pew. Just before reaching it Joseph passed them, and, opening the door, Mr. Henry

and Lawrie passed in, and he then placed
the books and retired to his own seat.

As soon as Mr. Henry appeared in the
churchyard he was most warmly and respectfully received by those assembled there,
and had not had time to receive half the
congratulations of his neighbours when the
vicar stopped them by his appearance.

Erect as usual, but with a trifle less
colour in his cheeks, Mr. Henry stood in
his family pew, holding Lawrie, whom he
had placed standing on the seat before
him, and encouraging him with his finger
to follow the service.

His responses were as clear and sonorous
as ever, especially after the prayer for
the Royal Family, and many of those
there assembled breathed a silent wish that
the kindly old gentleman might long live
to express his loyalty.

The Earl and his family occupied their
pew, to which they had a private entrance,

and they partook of the feeling, and shewed it by their kindly looks towards Mr. Henry's pew.

The example of Mr. Henry in interjecting his commentaries on the service was not lost upon Lawrie, who had some observations of his own to make upon the peculiarities of some of the people near him, and rather put Mr. Henry out of countenance by audibly commenting upon the big nose and loud snoring of an old farmer opposite to him, and loudly expressing a desire to awaken a little boy who sat on one of the free seats.

Service over, Mr. Henry waited until the greater part of the congregation had left, and, to his great satisfaction, found that the kind Earl was waiting at the door to have a chat with him.

Taking off his hat and for the moment exposing his fine old head, which the Earl insisted upon his immediately covering, he responded to the Earl's enquiries with innate taste and good breeding.

The Earl, noticing Lawrie, took him in his arms, and asked some questions about his being carried off by Basford, which he answered quite to Mr. Henry's satisfaction.

After dinner Lawrie began to wonder what he could play at.

Mr. Henry had fallen into a reverie connected with his dear sister, and Lawrie in vain looked into his face for some recognition, and failing that fell back upon Joseph, who, however, had on his "Sunday" face, which somehow or other was connected with a desire to have a quiet nap in the afternoon.

Lawrie was on the point of yawning, when Mattie, in her best, and looking what she really was, a good, honest, respectable servant girl, knocked at the door, and in reply to Mr. Henry's "Come in" entered, and, curtseying to Mr. Henry, said that she was going to take a walk, and made bold to ask if Master Lawrie would like to go with her, to which Mr. Henry gave a ready assent.

Gentle reader, is there anything vulgar in saying a word upon so well-worn a question as servants. I don't think myself there is, and with your leave will do so.

In the first place I may take it for granted that you admit how very essential it is to the comfort of a household that the servants should be " good," and that at the present day " good " servants are scarcely to be found.

Suppose we begin with the coachman.

If any one now-a-days, a candidate for that office, were to be asked if he could brew, he would be met with a " guffaw," and yet, in our younger days it was the duty of a coachman to brew the ale for the household, and we have a vivid recollection of the pure essence of malt and hops which, in our paternal mansion, the old coachman made twice a year (in March and October), and which more than one reverend divine would, on a hot summer's day, go some distance out of his way to imbibe.

The testing day for the last brew was usually an exciting occasion ; it took place at dinner, as soon as the first course had been handed round, and two or three friends, claiming to be connoisseurs, were usually invited to be present.

Enter the grey-haired coachman, whose service in the family has reached eighteen years, carrying a large tankard, topped with a cloud of foam. Holding the tankard in his right hand and a goblet in his left, he pours the frothing liquid into the well-poised cup. All eyes are fixed upon it. At first the fear is that it is a failure, as only a dull, creamy-looking fluid is seen in the goblet. In a few seconds a bright colour forms at the bottom, it increases gradually until a brilliant amber liquid, surmounted by a crest of foam, alone fills the goblet, and then follows the applause. The old man fills each glass at table, and the brew is pronounced first-rate, and all rejoice at knowing that the long range of " eighteens " in the cellar, destined for the next six months' consumption, will be in fine condition.

The customary sovereign is handed to the pleased old man, who, pulling his forelock, says, " God bless Master, Mistress, and all the family," and returns relieved from a load of anxiety.

Where will you find that affection for horses which arises from the fact that the old coachman bought them as colts, broke them in, and knows their temper and constitution as well as his own, and probably better.

Where is the coachman now-a-days that does not expect his percentage from the purveyor of forage? Who is there that does not complain of long bills for farrying and shoeing?

Why is it that he who keeps but two horses finds that he is continually told that the carriage can't be brought out, because one of the horses is ill?

If we were to take each other class of servant we might fill a volume on the subject.

We will content ourselves by saying generally, that "servant" is becoming synonymous with "low-class visitor," the object being to do as little work and expect as much indulgence in food, drink, and sleep as possible.

The disagreeables arising from this state of things fall principally upon the mistress of the house, her husband having his own occupation from home to attend to.

Many a poor wife goes to her bed at night broked-hearted with the harass she undergoes from her servants, and sees no relief from her troubles.

Is there no married man in the House of Commons who will try and grapple with this difficulty ?

Is it more important that a cabman, who does not enter your house, should be required to hold a licence, than that a servant, who has the custody of your children or the charge of your plate, or access to your jewellery, should be required to hold one ?

Why should not the servant registration system of France and Germany be applied to this country ?

The fact is that the cry for education is fast drying up the sources from which the servant class were formerly recruited, and shortly we shall be all " generals and no soldiers," and the sooner we meet the difficulty by calling in the " Chinee " the better.

Mattie Moore had been brought up by her mother in a thorough knowledge of household work, from nursing the baby upwards, and when she was seventeen she took a situation as under-nurse in the family of a rich Cheshire squire some miles from Whicham, to whom her father was well known.

She soon recommended herself to the family by her good conduct and truthfulness, and on the upper-nurse leaving about eighteen months afterwards, she was appointed in her place.

In all large establishments there will be one or more servants of indifferent character, but Mattie's discretion was such that she avoided contamination without giving offence, and was respected and esteemed by all the household.

She was beloved by her little charges,

and one little plump thing named Marian, about Lawrie's age, was a great pet with her.

A girl of such sterling worth, and withal very good-looking, does not usually wait long for an offer of marriage; and when she was twenty, a young farmer, whose father rented a good farm under the Earl, and who had known her from a child, asked her hand, and was accepted, and it was arranged that as soon as he could get a farm for himself they were to be married.

A few weeks before the date of our story, Farmer Cuthbertson, the young man's father, died suddenly, leaving his son a good round sum in cash and mortgages, and it was settled that Mattie should leave her situation and come home, and that, after a proper time from the father's death had expired, young Cuthbertson should take Mattie to his home as his wife.

The family in whose service she was were very sorry to lose so good a girl, but did not for an instant wish her stay beyond such time as would enable them to engage her successor, and this being effected, Mattie left, not only with the good wishes of everyone at the Hall, but with a great number of presents.

Her mistress gave her her wedding dress and bonnet and a becoming cloak, the young ladies found her in handkerchiefs, gloves, and many little etceteras. The young gentlemen bought her a nice clock for her sitting-room chimney-piece. The squire presented her with a ten-pound note. The butler and menservants clubbed together and bought her a handsomely-bound Bible, and the housekeeper and female servants contributed sufficient for a corresponding Prayer-book, both having a clasp with her name engraved on it.

So that when Mattie left she carried

with her her marriage " trousseau," and much affection and esteem as well.

Mr. Henry was aware of the impending marriage, and, when at Lumechester, had purchased for Mattie a handsome workbox, and gave it to her on his return home.

Master Lawrie's toilet being with some little difficulty completed, owing to the impatience of that young gentleman to proceed at once, Mattie took him by the hand and said that they would go into the park and see the squirrels hunting for the hazel nuts, and look at the swans on the water, and see the deer, all of which was very much to Lawrie's liking.

Shortly before they reached the gates of the park a young man, respectably dressed in mourning, about twenty-three, tall, good-looking, and with a manly bronzed face, overtook them, and shook Mattie's hand, and took off his hat to Master

Lawrie, and hoped he was quite well. He then gave his arm to Mattie, whilst Lawrie walked on the other side.

She distributed her conversation very fairly between her lover, it was young Cuthbertson, and Lawrie, so that the latter enjoyed his walk amazingly and was very loth to go home to his tea; but on Mattie representing that she had made a nice plum-cake for him he consented, and they returned homewards.

At the point where young Cuthbertson met Mattie they stopped, and they gave each other one hearty kiss and said good-bye.

On reaching home Lawrie ran into the dining-room, followed by Mattie, and, intimating to his godpapa that he had something important to tell him, stood on Mr. Henry's knees, and bent his head forward to his ear, and putting his mouth to it, and looking and laughing at Mattie like a very imp of mischief, whispered that he had seen Mattie "kiss a man;" and then leaning back, as if afraid that his assertion would not be accepted as true, he nodded twice to his godpapa, expressing in pantomime what would be expressed in French *C'est la verité vrai.*

Mattie knew what was coming and, with crimson face, had hurried towards the door, followed by Mr. Henry's "Oh! fie, Mattie," which made her almost cry, and when Lawrie ran to see where she was, she said, with a touch of vexation,—

"You naughty boy, I won't take you another walk with me;" when Lawrie jumped into her arms, and said that she ought not to kiss anybody but him. Upon this Mattie laughed, and Lawrie said if she would not be cross he wouldn't mind about her kissing a man, Joseph even, which made Mattie look vexed again.

The next Tuesday was fair-day at Cobford, a considerable town some miles from
Whicham.

Moore always attended this annual meet
of farmers, and it was arranged that he
and Mrs. Moore and Mattie should go to
it.

Lawrie begged so hard to go too that
Mr. Henry gave his consent, accompanying
it with a present of a crown, and a sly
hint before Mattie that he should be on
the look-out, and prevent Mattie giving
away any more kisses; whereupon the
scarlet came into Mattie's cheeks.

On the Tuesday, Moore, arrayed in his
Sunday suit, and looking the well-to-do
English farmer all over, and Mrs. Moore in
a silk dress, and looking a fit companion for
her husband, and Mattie with some pretty
new ribbons, and looking very nice and very
happy, and Lawrie, his little face as brown
as a berry, and clad in his velvet jacket

and vest, took their seats in the "trap"—
Moore and his wife in front, and the
other two at the back.

They started early, as Moore had to buy
some beasts for fattening, and, after a pleasant drive through the rich agricultural
scenery of Cheshire, they reached Cobford
and put up at the Farmers' Inn, and Moore
gave in his name for a place at the farmers'
dinner at one o'clock.

Mrs. Moore, Mattie, and Lawrie then left
him, the former to visit an old friend, and
Mattie with Lawrie to do some shopping
in anticipation of the all-important event
of her life, and then she and Lawrie were
to have some dinner at the old-established
confectioner's shop which monopolised the
custom of the ancient town.

They had arranged that all should meet
at the Farmers' Inn at four o'clock to start
homewards.

Before leaving her husband Mrs. Moore

said something to him in an undertone, whereupon Moore put on a "virtuous indignation" look, as if the something his wife had said conveyed an imputation for which there was not the slightest foundation, and he shook his head, indicating a negative with an air of intense seriousness.

Many years ago we saw in a picture gallery two paintings; one represented a portly husband, fresh from his toilet, and taking from his wife the latch-key proffered with one hand, whilst the forefinger of the other was lifted towards her husband's face as if warning him, and the husband's face had much the same kind of expression as Moore's bore.

The companion painting shewed the state of things on the return home, the post-prandial state presenting a strong contrast to the ante-prandial state. The hat on the back of the head, the necktie awry, the drunken leer, and the bent figure endeavouring to find the key-hole; whilst inside the house the clock points to half-past one, and the wife is seated shivering by the expiring embers of the fire.

Mrs. Moore, Mattie, and Lawrie were at the inn at four o'clock, but the horse was still in the stable, and the ostler said that he had not received - any orders to put it to.

Mrs. Moore sent message after message into the dinner-room, but in vain, and it began to get towards five o'clock.

At last a waiter came and told her that her husband would come home with Farmer Wright, a neighbour, in his trap, and that she and the other two must drive home without him.

Mrs. Moore heaved a deep sigh when the message was brought, and looked as if the weight of a mountain had been suddenly thrust upon her, but Mattie laughingly said,—

"Well, if father does want to enjoy himself in his own way on the only day in the year that he meets his friends why should he not? You need not trouble yourself, mother, about him ; he always has come home safe ever since I can recollect, and he'll come home safe with Wright this time."

Mrs. Moore, like many other good women, meant well, and was greatly attached to her husband ; but, like many other good and well-meaning women, was apt to seize upon a subject from a single point of view, and regard all other points of view as unworthy of notice ; and, moreover, she was somewhat actuated by that ambitious spirit which moves too many good and well-meaning women, viz., a desire to set up her own judgment as superior to that of her husband, and to try and lead instead of following—a great mistake, mesdames! The consequence was that occasionally a fractious spirit animated the two, and, notwithstanding their affection and respect for each other, produced an amount of irritation, and at times even a bitterness, which neither desired, and yet neither would avoid, when the fit was on them.

Moore considered his rights as a man infringed, and Mrs. Moore, for the moment, considered her rights as a woman trampled upon. It is only fair to Moore to say that he never began the fracas, and that he endured divers taunts and innuendos from his better half admirably up to a certain point, and had Mattie's hints and suggestions to her mother to " be quiet" been always listened to, nothing but a little letting-off of the steam would have ensued; but it was the womanly determination to have not only the last word, but the bitterest last word, that created an uncomfortableness in the house that lasted several days at least.

As regularly as the fair came round did Moore attend it, and whether he could not or would not, at all events he did not, explain to his wife that this particular day was the one on which he gained information to serve him all the following twelve months.

There were no local newspapers worth calling such, so there were no reports of agricultural meetings, no information on manuring, on seed-sowing, on stock-breeding, or the other many interesting topics for the farmer.

He knew perfectly well that, as soon might a toper expect welcome at a tea-party, as a farmer, who professed teetotalism, be cordially received at a farmer's meeting.

Mrs. Moore could not understand all this, but put down Moore's hints about its being " useful " to a preconceived determination to indulge in a debauch, to which Moore was as little prone in the common acceptation of the term as a man well could be. But, under this impression, she entered her annual protest against it with much the same effect as the late Mr. Joseph Hume, M.P., entered his annual protest against the budget.

But it had the effect at least that Moore, anticipating a " breeze " on his return home, frequently took on board more "Dutch courage " than he would have done had he felt sure that he would have been greeted with that considerate forbearance which does more to cure a fault than any amount of temper.

And after all what was there, as Mattie justly observed, to make a disturbance about? Her father invariably made and paid for his purchases before dinner, leaving himself no more money than would pay for a little jollity, and that in company with men of his own position, worthy

married men like himself. So while Mrs.
Moore's brows were dark Mattie's face was
full of hope for the best.

The Farmers' Inn was like all of its
class, roomy, somewhat gloomy, and with
a decidedly bucolic cast.

The dinner table groaned under huge
sirloins and immense saddles. A fine
haunch of venison was sure to be on the
table, a donation from the owner of
one of the neighbouring parks. Pudding
and custard followed in battalions, and
were succeeded by a monster cheese.
Tankards of strong ale were quaffed to
the health of His Majesty, and the neighbouring nobility and gentry. Then pipes
were called for, and half-hidden by a
canopy of smoke, the guests discussed the
prospects of the farmer and the politics of
the country.

The Lumechester meeting did not escape
notice, and on Moore mentioning the

adventure which befell Lawrie he became for the moment the most listened-to guest present.

He was beginning to enjoy himself when Mrs. Moore's message sounded on his ears like a "knell."

"Coming directly," he said, without the least intention of leaving; and, having repeated the same at intervals several times, he screwed up his courage to send Mrs. Moore the message that she was to go home without him.

Mrs. Moore took the reins and, being accustomed to driving, handled the ribbons' as well as Moore himself.

She was a little piqued at Mattie's taking her father's part, and dwelt dolefully upon the possibility of the farm becoming vacant through his sudden demise.

Tell me, gentle reader, which particular sex is pointed at in that large board set up close to the London and South-Western

Railway, not far from the Vauxhall-station, on which in the largest of all characters is announced that the advertiser undertakes funerals on the shortest notice, and at the lowest possible charges, adding, " Distance no object."

Assuming, for the sake of argument, that temptation is offered to each sex indiscriminately, permit us to enquire whether the distance is to be measured vertically or horizontally. Is it that there is not the least difficulty in placing one hundred miles between the dear departed one and the sorrowing survivor, or is it that the latter can, at his or her option, put an additional fifteen or twenty feet as an obstruction to a reappearance on this terrestrial globe ?

We have reason to know that the point is a knotty one, and has been the cause of more than one matrimonial difference, arising from the incidental raising of the question in the train.

They had proceeded rather more than half way when they espied a dark object lying in the road at some distance.

Mrs. Moore had slackened speed to talk to a farmer's son from near Whicham, who was walking home, and seeing the object, and some yards beyond it a laden cart with a pair of horses motionless, she had a kind of foreboding of evil, and pulling up asked the young man to go forward and see what it was.

He reached it, and threw himself on his knees by the side of the object, with up-lifted hands, and there remained.

They drove slowly towards him. He was kneeling over his dying brother. The latter had been to the fair, had got intoxicated, and driving his cart had fallen under the wheels, which had passed over his chest, and life was fast ebbing.

By this time others had come up, and

they drew the dying man to the bank on the side of the road.

As Mrs. Moore drove by, Mattie tried to hide the sight from Lawrie by covering his head with a shawl, but through an opening the boy saw for the first time the " Angel of Death."

CHAPTER XIII.

GREEN, having arrested Basford, shewed every consideration for him and kindness to his wife. It was his duty to take him, that done, his natural kindliness, nay, even chivalry, for brave men are ever chivalrous, came into play, and saying,—

"Richard Basford, I know that thou art a good though a misguided man, give me thy word that thou wilt not attempt to escape, and I will not make thee feel thy capture."

Basford gave his word.

Giving them a little time to dress and collect their things, Green descended the ladder, followed by his prisoner, Mary Basford, and Jem, and in the dead of the night they passed through the village, not meeting a single person, and arrived at the valley and went to the inn.

The occupants had long gone to rest, but Green, prepared for the emergency, had a short note ready, and as the landlord appeared at the window, the lithe and nimble Jem, who had climbed a rain spout, handed it to him.

The burning rushlight was sufficient to allow the landlord to decipher that the writer had the authority of His Most Gracious Majesty King George the Third, and accordingly, though very scantily attired, he descended, and admitted, to his surprise, the farm labourer. He was at first inclined to treat it as rather too practical a joke, but on Green shewing his warrant his manner changed altogether.

Green required accommodation for all the

party, and this the landlord was able to provide, and also a carriage the next morning to Crosdale.

He enjoined the landlord not to disclose his relation to Basford, of whom he spoke highly; and the landlord, all of whose sympathies were in favour of the just rights of labour, treated Basford and his wife with much kindness, and when they left shook them heartily by the hand, and wished them well out of their troubles.

On the road to Crosdale, Green amused them much by his account of the capture of the "soldier," and said how he won over the gaolers by his frank, soldier-like ways, and how open-handed he was—for the money found upon him was not all the produce of his robberies— and how he seemed to have been a very "Claude Duval" in his treatment of females whom he met in the company of his victims; how on one occasion he had met a young man and his *fiancée*, who were going with their savings to a neighbouring bank to put them on deposit, and with them go into a little business; and how the girl pleaded her cause and that of her intended husband with so much power that although he held every farthing they possessed, he generously returned the whole amount, and added a guinea of his own for a wedding-ring.

Then Basford told him of his leap for life, and where he landed, and how he had got on the barge, and spoke feelingly of the kindness of the bargee and his wife.

Green did not speak of his adventure with the bargee, and how completely he had been done.

Jem was seated on the box by the side of the driver, and, being free from anxiety as to the success of the journey, enjoyed the scenery amazingly, and the driver gave the names of the principal mountains, and told him a good deal about the people and their primitive ways.

Arrived at Crosdale, Green decided to remain there all night, as the night before had been mostly occupied in the arrest of Basford and the journey on foot from St. Peter's in the Rocks.

Here Jem drew Green on one side, and asked him if he would allow him to leave and go to Drawbridge, and join him in a couple of days at Lunechester.

Jem held his cap in his left hand whilst making the request, and twirled it nervously round, and when Green's quick eye led him to suspect something, Jem let out a word or two about a little girl whose brother had asked him to dinner.

This was enough to give Green an idea of the state of the case, and he at once consented.

"But Jem," said he, "there's one thing I would like to settle with thee at once."

"What's that?" said Jem.

" Well," proceeded Green, "thou know'st that Government have offered a reward of £100 for taking Basford, and it will be a question between thee and me how much I am to have and how much thou.

" Now, Jem, I'll be fair and above-board with thee. I shall say that thou, not being a constable, art not entitled to anything more than thy day's pay as an " extra," but some Government fellow may write down and make a fuss and say that a poor factory lad must have a fair part, and what that fair part may be he'll take twelve months to consider, and meantime neither thee nor I get anything, but Government keeps all, and God knows when either of us will be paid."

" So I'll tell thee what I'll do. I'll pay thee twenty pounds down for thy chance ; so take it or not as thou likest."

Jem had heard of the reward being

offered, but never dreamt of getting any
part of it, for the reason Green gave ; so he
said,—

"Mr. Green, I don't want to take anything from thee that I haven't a right to.
Thou hast run Basford to cover, and I can't
rightly say that I should have anything ; so
take it all thysel."

"No," said Green, "thou art a good lad,
Jem, and a brave one, and I respect thee,"
giving him his hand, "and I think that
between man and man what I offer is but
fair, and there are five sovereigns towards
the bargain, and may they do thee much
good."

Five bright golden sovereigns! Jem never
dreamt even of such a sum being lawfully
fingered by himself.

"Five sovereigns, Mr. Green," he said
(taking breath after the word " sovereigns"),
" its too much, sir—and fifteen more to
follow."

And then he thought he could go to Lilian's mother, a rich man, and ask to "keep company" with her daughter, and tears of joy came into his eyes, and he said,—

" Thank you, Mr. Green ; if you say it's right, I'm content," and thereupon Jem took up the sovereigns, having just examined the pocket in which he was about to put them to see there was no hole in it, and walked to the cottage where he had put up before, a richer and a better man.

The following morning, Green and Mr. and Mrs. Basford left by coach for Lumechester, first saying a cordial good-bye to Jem, who, owing to what Green had said about him, had created a favourable impression on Basford and his wife.

On arriving at Lumechester, Basford was taken to the gaol, and on entering it shed tears, which his wife seeing, exclaimed,—

"Richard, thou art not the Basford of past times to shed tears. Wait until thy own conscience tells thee thou hast done wrong?"

Basford felt the justice of the rebuke, though in reality he was mourning over the sudden stop put to the pleasant dreams of a country life in which he and his wife had been indulging.

She parted from him at the gate of the prison, first thanking Green heartily for his kindness on their journey, and then, embracing her husband, gave vent to loud sobs, which he in his turn checked, telling her to place her confidence in the Almighty, who, he doubted not, would see justice done to him.

As she understood that it would be several days before she would be permitted to see her husband, she made her way home to Drawbridge, but with a heart full of sorrow.

On parting from his fellow-traveller at Crosdale, Jem went round the town and looked in the shop windows for something to buy for Lilian, and seeing a nice pin-cushion covered with crimson velvet and bordered round with sea shells he bought it. Then he shouldered his bundle, and took the route to Drawbridge, which he had traversed but a few days before.

What was it that quickened the boy's pace, so that the rough road seemed smooth? Was it Lilian's face that again peered over every brake, looked at him from the depths of every stream, and danced on the lonely moors?

Very weary he reached the suburbs of Drawbridge late in the evening. It had been a beautiful day and the evening corresponded, followed by a warm night.

He knew no one in Drawbridge and felt a difficulty about the question of bed. He therefore determined to camp out all night.

He turned into a roadside inn and got some simple refreshment, and then sought a soft place in the opposite field, concealed by rising ground from the road, and fell asleep and dreamt of Lilian.

He went to the same roadside inn in the morning and got his breakfast, and asked the ostler to lend him the "wherewith" for his ablutions,' and Jem spent some time in arranging his hair, but not quite the two hours devoted by some youths of fashionable proclivities to their back hair.

This finished, Jem took the way to Lilian's mother, and he thought it best to go there after the mill had opened and Lilian's brother was at his work.

He knocked at the door with trembling hand. It was opened by Mrs. Bowthrop, and Jem was rather surprised that she did not instantly recognize him; but the outdoor exercise and pure air of the hills since he first saw him had much changed his complexion, and, from being almost ashy pale, it had assumed a healthy hue and he looked quite a different lad. Taking off his hat, he said,—

"Hope you won't feel offended, ma'am, but I've brought Miss Lilian a little present, because her brother gave me my dinner the other day," and with that produced the pincushion.

"Why," said Mrs. Bowthrop, "it's the factory boy, but he does look so much better. Come in, lad." So he entered; and who should come from the back room immediately but Lilian.

"Why, bless the boy," exclaimed Mrs. Bowthrop, "he's ill again." Jem turned deadly pale, and Lilian took his hand and made him sit down.

Jem said, "I'm not ill indeed, but I feel how kind you are to speak so nice to a poor factory lad, and Miss Lilian, I've brought a little thing that I bought at Crosdale for you ; maybe you'll not say no."

Lilian took the little present and admired it very much, and Jem's simple way of saying that he had bought it for her quite won her heart.

And what female's pride is not flattered by having something bought for her, and what female's hand is not ready to receive that something ?

Is not " buying something " a true and certain criterion of devoted affection on the part of the buyer, and the receipt thereof a sure and certain token on the part of the recipient of great affection for the giver ?

A'hem ; we fear not, though we regret to say, as regards the latter, that it is generally considered a safe indication thereof.

Does not the enamoured squire in the

" School for Scandal " measure his adored one's attachment to him thus:

"Oh, she is so fond of me, she's always asking me to buy her something?"

Oh, ye members of my own sex, why not imitate the example of the great Marlborough, and whilst impressing a devoted kiss on the lips of the girl you love, gently disentangle the diamond necklace from the white neck.

Mrs. Bowthrop asked the boy to stay and see her son, and take some dinner.

Jem sat down in the little parlour, and Lilian joined him, and noticed how much better he looked, and as they talked she liked Jem's sensible observations.

Then she asked him where he had been that he seemed so much stronger, and he told her; and she was quite interested with his account of the Valley and Saint Peter's in the Rocks and the festival, and began to think that he was quite a traveller, and had a great deal of courage to go to such places by himself; for Jem said nothing as to his companion.

And when he found that she took quite an interest in his proceedings, he produced the five sovereigns Green had given him, and ranged them on the table in a row, and said that he had " come into some money," and that he was to have fifteen more in a few days.

Lilian's eyes fairly glistened as she saw the golden treasure spread out before her.

Pizarro's heart could not have beat quicker than hers when Montezuma caused the room in his palace, selected by the Spanish warrior, to be piled up with gold to the ceiling.

" And is that all your own, Jem ? " Lilian called him Jem for the first time, and did not a thrill of pleasure rush through the boy's frame when she did so.

" Its all mine," said Jem, " and honestly come by."

Whereupon Lilian went into the back room and brought her mother to look at the money, and told her that Jem had fifteen pounds more coming to him, and Jem repeated to Mrs. Bowthrop that it was all " honestly come by."

The latter looked him steadily in the face, and, seeing that the boy met her gaze without the slightest flinching. she believed him, and said,—

" Jem," this was the first time that she had called him "Jem" also; " that is a good deal of money for a boy like you to have, and you must take care that nobody cheats you out of it. You will find it very useful some day."

Stephen Bowthrop then came in for his dinner, and seeing Jem there with five sovereigns lying on the table, and Lilian's face much flushed, and his mother's usually placid countenance with a touch of excitement in it, he could not tell what to make of it.

He gave Jem his hand, and, like the others, was struck with his improved looks, and said,

"Where have you been, lad; you look made over again?"

So Jem explained, and seeing Stephen's eyes directed to the gold, he added,—

"I've come in for some money."

And then Lilian took up the story and said how much more he had got, "and all honestly come by, Steve," she added.

Stephen looked rather serious, which Jem observing said, "Thou need not be afraid, there's a gentleman in Lumechester, Mr. Green is his name, knows all about it, and thou canst write to him if thou likes; that's where he lives," handing Stephen Green's private address, "and he has to give me t'other fifteen pounds when I get to Lumechester."

This quite satisfied Stephen, and the little party became very friendly, and Lilian sat by Jem's side at dinner and helped him to the dishes before them.

When Stephen rose to return to the mill, he said,—

"Jem, you had better stay here until to-morrow ; a good night's rest in a bed will do you good."

Jem had told them about his camping out all night, and readily accepted the invitation, and Mrs. Bowthrop put a turn-up bed in Stephen's room, with nice clean sheets for him. He was very glad to rest himself after the long walk of the day before, and sat in Mrs. Bowthrop's parlour listening to the canary and looking at the books in the book-case, and was absorbed in " Robinson Crusoe" when Mrs. Bowthrop and Lilian, having finished the housework, brought their sewing, and sat down for a chat with him.

Mrs. Bowthrop told him all about Sussex, and the big farms and well-kept hedges, and that there was no manufacturing going on, and that the air was free from smoke, and that almost every cottage had its little flower-garden in front, and that the cottagers vied with each other in having fine roses and fuschias, and that many of them had vines clustering over the doors and creeping round the windows, loaded with grapes in the autumn, from which they made a delicious wine.

We can ourselves vouch as to the latter, for have we not drank it at Bamber, and pronounced it equal to the " Catawba " of the Ohio valley, of which Americans are so proud.

Mrs. Bowthrop noticed a suspicious-looking bump on Jem's temple, and asked him if he had met with an accident.

Jem was rather surprised at the question, and for a moment scarcely knew what to say, but then replied,—

"Why, ma'am, it was only me and a butcher's boy at Crosdale had a 'set to.'

"A set to," said Mrs. Bowthrop, "what do you mean by a 'set to?'"

"Why, I fowt him, and licked him," said Jem, with emphasis.

Mrs. Bowthrop put down her sewing and looked at the boy.

"What!" she said; "do you mean you've been fighting?"

"Yoi," said Jem, in a matter of fact way, as if there was nothing unusual in it.

Lilian laughed heartily at her mother's expression of amazement, and at Jem's cool admission, and asked him if he had ever fought before.

Thereupon Jem mentioned a few of his recent passages at arms, and the more Mrs. Bowthrop looked astonished at his quarrelsome character, as unblushingly admitted by himself, the more Lilian laughed, and admired the brave spirit of the boy.

But when Jem proceeded to narrate one encounter in which, finding that his adversary was feeling about uncomfortably for his nose, Jem, to save that organ, seized his opponent's ear and bit off a piece, which settled the fight in his favour, Mrs. Bowthrop could contain herself no longer.

"Oh dear! oh dear! oh dear! I've often heard that the 'Sheere' people were cruel, but I never did think they were half so cruel as that," and suiting the action to the words she lifted her hands up and then put them down on her knees, looking at Jem as if, in her opinion, he had committed all but murder.

Lilian roared with laughter, looking first at Jem's imperturbable face, and then at her mother's full of horror, and was almost choked when Mrs. Bowthrop asked what he did with the piece of ear, and he coolly replied, "Put it in a bottle with some spirits of wine, and it's on my chimney-piece now."

In the evening Stephen came home and they had tea, and a pleasant chat, and Stephen laughed heartily at Lilian's account of Jem's fighting propensities, and her mother's amazement, and thought all the better of Jem; for he knew by that time quite enough of the Lancashire youths to know that it was almost impossible to keep them off fighting, and told his mother that as that was the case it was far better to come off first rather than second best.

Still Mrs. Bowthrop had her misgivings about the matter, and inclined to the secret opinion that to marry her daughter to such a man would be like giving young Cinderella as wife to the King of the Cannibal Islands.

Jem said he must leave for Lumechester the next day, and, accordingly, the next morning, when Stephen went to his work, Jem prepared to leave but stayed behind to pack up his bundle. He shook hands with

Mrs. Bowthrop, who was putting away the breakfast things in the kitchen, and Lilian, closing the door, followed him to the front door, and Jem, stopping for a moment, scarcely knowing how to say good-bye to her, she put out her hand, and said, smiling, "Good-bye, Jem."

Jem took her hand, and looking in her face felt very confused.

"Good-bye, Jem," she said again, laughing, and putting her face a little forward. Jem put his lips to hers, and for the first time drank at the eternal spring.

CHAPTER XIV.

BEST INTENTIONS OUT OF PLACE.

THE Rev. Erasmus Godwin accepted
with much pleasure the invitation of Mr.
and Mrs. Robert to visit them, for it
fitted in very conveniently with a request
which he had received from the trustees
of the Barport Sunday-schools to preach
the annual sermon in aid of the funds for
their support.

This was a high and distinguished
honour, for the Barport Sunday-schools
were a model of their kind, and the
scholars were numbered by thousands, and
the Independents justly prided themselves
on their excellent management and beneficial effect.

When, therefore, the Rev. Erasmus Godwin received the important missive requesting him to undertake the service upon which the trustees relied so much for filling their coffers for the coming year, he determined to rise to the occasion, and preach a sermon which should be in every way worthy of himself and the cause.

He dimly shadowed forth to his wife the nature and extent of the discourse which it was his intention to deliver, and having, in his own mind, separated the subject into nineteen heads, with occasional subsidiary divisions, he committed the whole to paper, and exhibited the ponderous mass with guileless joy to his better half.

Now she, being a practical woman, ventured to suggest that if he was going to preach all that " she scarcely knew how they would find time for the collection ; " for it struck her that a good collection would be more gratifying to the trustees than any sermon, however long.

But her worthy husband by no means saw it in that light. It was past his conception that filthy lucre could for a moment be deemed by the guardians of the religious education of the youths of Barport a substitute for the telling appeals to sinners contained in the nineteen heads of his discourse. No! he repudiated such an idea, and felt, no doubt, that the nineteen heads would produce such convictions in the minds of the stray sheep of Barport as would be an ample substitute for any deficiency in the school funds.

He permitted his wife to pack up his valise, but no hands save his own were permitted to touch the precious manuscript. It was carefully enclosed in two covers of white paper, and a third cover of strong brown paper, on which was written, " The Rev. Erasmus Godwin," in large characters.

When the coach which did the branch service between Severnworth and Hampton-Bare, where it caught up the line of coaches between London and the North, stopped at his door, the worthy pastor was evidently deeply in the midst of the nineteen heads, the parcel containing which he held tightly clasped under his left arm ; but he heard not the sound of Tom's bugle, as that civil coachman blew a loud blast to announce his arrival, and was only roused from his reverie by his wife taking him by the arm rather sharply and telling him the coach was at the door.

He only looked at the parcel under his arm, and seeing that safe was content, and was about to get into the coach without his valise, which his wife sent after him by a servant.

Mrs. Godwin had divers misgivings about the future fate of the valise, seeing

how utterly indifferent he was to all
sublunary affairs.

Arrived at Hampton-Bare there were
three or four coaches drawn up opposite
to the booking-office. Tom took the valise
out of the boot, and placed it in the boot
of the coach by which he understood Mr.
Godwin would travel northward.

The latter, however, with the nineteen
heads, got into a coach which was starting
eastward, and it was not until Tom going
to the right coach for his customary
shilling, which Mr. Godwin in his abstrac-
tion had forgotten to give him, discovered
that Mr. Godwin was not inside.

Begging the coachman to wait a moment,
he went and looked inside the other coaches,
and found Mr. Godwin in a deep reverie,
and roused him by first asking for his
shilling, and then informing him that he
was in the wrong coach.

Mr. Godwin laid down the parcel on

the seat to get a shilling out of his pocket
for Tom, and then, the latter telling him
that he had not a moment to spare, jumped
out of the coach, and rushed into the right
one just before the horses started.

Scarcely had they done so, when Mr.
Godwin discovered that he had left the
nineteen heads behind him in the other
coach, and frantically calling to the coachman to stop, he got out and forgot his valise,
and although he instantly discovered his
loss, shouting had no effect; for the driver,
behind his time, had dashed off at a slap-
ping pace. He hurried as hard as he could
to the booking-office, and to his horror
found that the coach, with the nineteen
heads, had also left.

A sympathising ostler standing outside
recommended a chaise and pair to overtake
the latter, but Mr. Godwin hesitated at the
expense of a pair, and ordered a horse
and gig, after first receiving the ostler's

assurance that he would be able to over-take the coach in a quarter of an hour.

But although the coach, like a will-o'-the-wisp, was always on the point of being overtaken, yet by some extraordinary fatuity, the secret of which seemed well known to the driver, it never did overtake the coach, and all Mr. Godwin's shouting to the coach when they got in sight of it, and waving his pocket-handkerchief tied to the end of his umbrella, had not the least effect, and they drove into the same yard immediately after the arrival of the coach.

Mr. Godwin appeared just in time. There being no address on the parcel, the coach-man assumed it was destined for the town the coach stopped at, and had just handed it to a helper about the stables, directing him to find out " the parson " whose name it bore, and to demand a shilling for the carriage, and something for himself.

Addressing the coachman, Mr. Godwin asked for the parcel, and to his horror was told that he had just started off a lad with it.

"How long ago?" said Mr. Godwin.

"Just a minute," was the reply.

"In which direction?" said Mr. Godwin, anxiously.

"Turn to the left, then to the right, and then go straight on."

Did Mr. Godwin run? Well, not quite; but he certainly exhibited considerable pedestrian powers, and managed to get in sight of a youth with a brown paper parcel, who fortunately stopped to have a longing gaze in a pastry-cook's window, and so allowed Mr. Godwin to get up to him.

"You've got a parcel," said the former, much out of breath.

"Yes," said the helper, "it's for a parson."

"It is mine," said Mr. Godwin.

"Maybe," replied the youth, "but I don't know that."

The sight, however, of the shilling, and sixpence for himself, overcame his scruples, and he handed the parcel to Mr. Godwin.

The nineteen heads being safe, what mattered the valise? Probably had Mrs. Godwin been asked the question she would have answered that it mattered more than the nineteen heads; for over them she had had no anxiety, but in nicely arranging the valise she had had a good deal.

There he stood for a few minutes in a reverie. Dear good soul, his face was lighted up with joy, and in imagination he was standing before a vast congregation, listening, spell bound, to his sermon.

He was roused from his trance by a touch on the shoulder. It was the driver of the gig, who had a double object in view, and had followed Mr. Godwin when he left the yard.

The first was to get his fare, and the second was to secure Mr. Godwin as a back fare.

Mr. Godwin paid ten shillings for the ten miles, and half-a-crown the driver's fee. The latter then said that he had just been asked by a " commercial " to drive him to Hampton-Bare at one shilling a mile, but he preferred taking his first fare at sixpence and the driver's fee.

Mr. Godwin was in too abstracted a state to enquire about the coach, which always returned in an hour after its arrival, and closed the bargain at once, though for one-third of the expense he could have returned by the coach in less time.

Had the telegraph been in use when Mr. Godwin discovered the loss of the nineteen heads what time and expense he would have saved.

What fortunate beings we are to possess thee, thou marvellous telegraph! Had'st

thou been known to the ancient Romans
they would have embodied thee in god-
like form in marble ; a vast temple would
have been raised to thine honour ; priests
in gorgeous robes would have offered sacri-
fices at thine altar, and victors would have
laid spoils at thy feet! Miraculous agent
for good, wondrous for evil! Thou followest
the track of armies, and blowest the bubbles
of the Bourse ; thou carriest the winged
message through Alpine snows and the
silent recesses of the ocean ; thou art the
swift bearer of the news that gladdens, and
of that which pierces, the heart ; thou art
the great annihilator of time and space.
Thou art the lightning of the gods transformed into the language of men.

On Mr. Godwin's arrival at Hampton-
Bare, he managed, but with some difficulty,
to get his seat transferred to the coach
of the next day.

He knew the Independent Minister at

Hampton-Bare, and called upon him, bringing his parcel, and was requested by the latter to take up his quarters with him, an offer thankfully accepted.

This was an opportunity not to be lost. Here at least was one who could appreciate the nineteen heads and all their subdivisions.

Accordingly, after tea, Mr. Godwin untied his parcel. He then explained to his brother (Mr. White was the minister's name) the great occasion at Barport, and the vast thought and midnight labour he had bestowed upon the sermon.

Then unfolding the ponderous manuscript, he requested brother White to be so kind as to listen while he read over what he called a skeleton sermon, and the former willingly acceded to his request.

Mr. Godwin then commenced, and as he proceeded warmed up with his subject, and had no more thought of brother White than if he had not been present.

One hour had elapsed and still no signs of finishing.

The second hour passed, and still the worthy soul, wrapt in his subject, continued reading as if he had a most attentive listener.

At last the nineteenth head was reached, and then the "finally," and Mr. Godwin, raising his eyes to see the effect upon brother White, found that he was fast asleep.

Poor Mr. Godwin! He never suspected for a moment that it was the sermon which had produced this effect on brother White —that was simply impossible. He attributed it to over exertion during the day, and pitied him for having missed hearing one of the most exhaustive sermons ever composed.

Brother White was awoke by the ces-

sation of Mr. Godwin's voice, and, in some
confusion, begged his guest's pardon for
having given way to a momentary weakness of the flesh, and thanked him for
his learned exposition of the text he had
chosen, which gave some comfort to the
mind of Mr. Godwin, as showing that it
was not all, but only part, of the discourse
which he had missed.

Mr. Godwin folded up the nineteen heads,
and, as brother White looked on, the latter
drily observed that it might be well for his
brother to consider whether the collection
should not be made before the sermon, a
hint entirely unnoticed by Mr. Godwin,
whose simple mind could not compass the
idea of a sermon being too long.

The following morning Mr. Godwin left
by the coach for Lumechester. It was a
lovely day, and he elected to take a seat
on the top behind the coachman, who was
radiant in a green coat with brass buttons,

and a spray of flowers in a buttonhole. As
they left Hampton Bare the guard blew a
lively blast from his bugle; the coachman
shewed his skill as a whip by touching his
leader's ears with the end of the whip-cord ;
and the horses, well-bred and coats shining
like velvet, bounded away as if they had
a feather weight behind them.

As the dashing "Tally-ho" whirled
through the streets, the female portion of
the community rushed to the windows,
and the small boys hurrahed.

Clear of the town the coachman lessened
his speed, to the great relief of Mr. Godwin, who was in a state of extreme nervous
excitement whilst passing through it.

If a ragged young urchin, defying
danger, was about to rush across the street
in front of the horses, Mr. Godwin would
implore the coachman to pull up, and, as
the adventurous youth landed safely on the
opposite side, and stood grinning at the

coachman, Mr. Godwin would shake his head at him, and express strong disapproval.

But when he saw a carter deliberately draw his cart across the road in front of the leaders, his indignation knew no bounds. He stood upright, the coach being brought to a full stop, and using the coachman's hat like a pulpit-cushion, he emphatically denounced such a proceeding and temporarily deprived the coachman of his power of vision.

In whirling round a corner he would bring all his weight to bear to counteract the tendency to deviate from the centre of gravity, and so pressed upon a very stout party who sat next to him, that the former asked him if he was in the insurance line, and had granted a policy on the coach.

The language of the horse-keepers, at every change of horses, was strongly comdemned by him, and he earnestly exhorted them to forsake their evil ways, and was not without hope that he had made a strong impression upon them.

In fact, from the beginning to the end of the journey Mr. Godwin exercised such an amount of watchfulness over the lives and limbs of the passengers that the coachman and guard christened him " The Special Interposition."

During all this time the parcel never forsook its place under the arm of Mr. Godwin, even under the greatest excitement, for if he extended one arm the other remained on duty. At last, after many hours of travel, they reached Barport, the last stopping place before getting to the end of their journey.

From the top of the coach Mr. Godwin gazed fondly on the large building in which on the following Sunday it would be his pride to unfold to a rivetted audience the nineteen heads and their sub-divisions.

Here a special team were put into the coach; big, well-bred horses, groomed and harnessed to perfection, and guaranteed to do the last seven miles in a little more than half-an-hour.

They left Barport at a great pace, and were all in high spirits at being so near the end of the journey, when suddenly they all felt the coach roll as if losing its balance, each roll being worse than the last, when one final and terrible roll sent the mass over with a crash.

A dreadful scene of confusion ensued.

The leaders kicked and plunged, and finally broke away and disappeared in the distance.

The wheelers were thrown one on the top of the other, and kicked and struggled furiously.

The coachman lay on the ground in-

sensible, grasping the reins in his left hand
and the whip in his right.

The guard, though bleeding from a
wound on the temple, threw off his coat
and held the horses down by their
heads.

The passengers were pitched in all di-
rections.

Mr. Godwin stuck manfully to the parcel,
and, grasping it with both hands, was
deposited on the body of his stout neighbour, who received the concussion in anything but a submissive spirit, and, in fact
broadly accused Mr. Godwin with causing
the upset by worrying and interfering with
the driver, a charge which hurt his feelings much.

The road being one of great traffic
assistance was speedily at hand.

Some of the passengers were seriously
injured, and were carried off to Barport
Infirmary, the others resumed their places

on the coach, which was driven into Lumechester with a pair only.

Gentle reader, did you ever cross the Pyrennees and Guadaramma mountains to Madrid before the opening of the railway dispensed with the Diligence service?

What would have become of the Rev. Erasmus Godwin had he been seated in the banquette of a Diligence on that route we know not.

Mountain gorges, yawning precipices, huge boulders lying across the road; deep streams where the water at the ford rose to above the mule's bellies; descents where all the wheels were locked and the Diligence seemed inclined to turn a somersault; and yet the little monkey of a driver sent his mules down at full speed, and we once saw the whole thirteen rolled over in a heap on the top of each other.

There was something sensational in

crossing those vast mountain ranges in those days, the eagle soaring above, and his confrère, the bandit, ranging below.

END OF VOL. II.

PRINTED BY THE CHARING CROSS PUBLISHING COMPANY, LIMITED,
5, FRIAR STREET, BROADWAY, LONDON, E.C

www.ingramcontent.com/pod-product-compliance
Lightning Source LLC
Chambersburg PA
CBHW030348270326
41926CB00009B/1010